THE BOOK OF
Wizard Craft

In Which the Apprentice Finds Spells, Potions, Fantastic Tales & 50 Enchanting Things to Make

LARK BOOKS

A Division of Sterling Publishing Company, Inc.

NEW YORK

AUTHORS
Janice Eaton Kilby
Deborah Morgenthal
Terry Taylor

ILLUSTRATION
Lindy Burnett

ART DIRECTOR
Susan McBride

ASSISTANT EDITOR
Veronika Alice Gunter

EDITORIAL ASSISTANTS
Roper Cleland
Emma Jones

ASSISTANT ART DIRECTOR
Hannes Charen

TECHNICAL ILLUSTRATION
Orrin Lundgren

Library of Congress Cataloging-in-Publication Data

Kilby, Janice Eaton, 1955-
    The Book of Wizard Craft: In Which the Apprentice Finds Spells,
Potions, Fantastic Tales, and 50 Enchanting Things to Make /Janice
Eaton Kilby, Deborah Morgenthal, and Terry Taylor.

p. cm

ISBN 1-57990-206-5 (Hardcover) ISBN 1-57990-284-7 (paperback)

10 9 8 7 6 5

Published by Lark Books, a division of
Sterling Publishing Co., Inc.
387 Park Avenue South
New York, N.Y. 10016

© 2001, Lark Books

Distributed in Canada by Sterling Publishing,
c/o Canadian Manda Group, One Atlantic Ave., Suite 105
Toronto, Ontario, Canada M6K 3E7

Distributed in Australia by Capricorn Link (Australia) Pty Ltd.,
P.O. Box 704, Windsor, NSW 2756, Australia

Distributed in the U.K. by Guild of Master Craftsman Publications Ltd.,
Castle Place 166 High Street, Lewes, East Sussex, England, BN7 1XU.
Tel: (+44) 1273 477374 • Fax: (+44) 1273 478606
Email: pubs@thegmcgroup.com • Web: www.gmcpublications.com

The written instructions, photographs, designs, patterns, and projects in
this volume are intended for the personal use of the reader and may be
reproduced for that purpose only. Any other use, especially commercial
use, is forbidden under law without written permission of the copyright
holder.

Every effort has been made to ensure that all the information in this
book is accurate. However, due to differing conditions, tools, and individual skills, the publisher cannot be responsible for any injuries, losses,
and other damages that may result from the use of the information in
this book.

If you have questions or comments about this book, please contact:
Lark Books
50 College Street
Asheville, North Carolina 28801
(828) 253-0467

Printed in China

Acknowledgments

It's been a wonder and a marvel to work with all of our collaborators on *The Book of Wizard Craft*. Thank you, Rob Pulleyn and Carol Taylor, for giving even our wildest ideas your blessing. Something more than chance brought us Susan McBride, with her uniquely gifted eye and sensitive heart, to art direct this book. Illustrator Lindy Burnett created her inspired art because she shared a deep understanding of our intent. And finally, we'd like to thank every writer, artist, and explorer for showing us again and again that curiosity and open-mindedness are the true ingredients for making magic.

I also want to give my love and thanks to Tip, Angela, and Ryan Kilby for sharing wizardly ideas and enthusiasms with me. JEK

Thanks to my parents who never discouraged me from making things—even when they weren't quite sure what I was doing. TBT

A special thank you to my daughter, Corrina, who reminds me to look closely at things and find the magic in the flower, the spider, and the smooth stone. DM

CONTENTS

HOW THIS BOOK CAME TO BE,

& What You Can Do With It

Imagine that late one night you get a phone call from a gentleman who asks you to help him write a book that shares all the magical knowledge he's gathered—and by the way, he's been working on it for the last 600 years! That's exactly what happened to us. He told us that he'd been compiling a notebook for centuries, intending to pass it on to a deserving young wizard-in-training after he retired. When the Wizard realized he could reach millions of young wizards and sorceresses by publishing his notebook, he decided to call us so we could help him turn these notes into a first-of-its-kind book. Fine, we thought, how hard could that be? Well, we'll tell you…

First of all, during some of our meetings, the Wizard completely vanished but kept right on talking. Other times he turned into a griffin or an oak tree. As you can imagine, this took some getting used to. And deciphering his notes was quite a challenge. Some sections were hard to read because of all the mice footprints; other pages were splotched with goo and slime from alchemy experiments gone wild. Not to mention the hundreds of cobwebs covering his lab equipment. And the

foot-long rats and singing beetles scampering over everything! But we persevered, and the more we read and talked, the more excited we got!

The Book of Wizard Craft contains the Wizard's own recipes and instructions for making more than 50 of his most useful tools and potions, including a real wizard's robe and hat, a crystal ball, magic wands, flying carpets, high-speed chase brooms, rings of power, secret journals, apothecary ingredients, such as mandrake root and dragon's blood, etc. You name it, the Wizard tells you how to make it in this book. He also shared his *Spooky Foods Cookbook* and his *Really Useful Book of All-Good Magic Spells, Cheering Charms, and Divination* with us, and we put those in, too.

It also became clear to us that the Wizard has known practically everyone in the magical arts, and many famous nonwizards for the last several centuries. He has a great sense of humor and had some wonderful stories to tell, so we asked him to write them down too. All the important legends and myths, the real stuff of centuries of wizard lore, are here for you to read. And the Wizard himself wrote the Foreword and

Farewell for the book. Made us a bit teary-eyed, they did.

A couple of cautions are in order, so pay attention! First of all, use your common sense! Don't eat or drink any of the potions or project ingredients, and be very careful with sharp tools. **If you see this spider next to a how-to project, you MUST stop and go find an adult wizard or nonwizard to help you.** We mean it, sincerely! Otherwise, the Wizard told us he will come back and personally turn you into a toad. Or at the very least, you'll be in really big trouble.

We hope you enjoy reading this book, and that you have lots of fun making all these wonderful, wizardly things! Please don't write to us asking how you can contact the Wizard, though. We had to promise never to divulge his name or his location, never ever. And in the wizard world, a promise made is a promise kept.

Janice Eaton Kilby

Deborah Morgenthal

Terry B. Taylor

FOREWORD by the Wizard

After 600 years, the time has come for me to share what I know of wizard craft, and it is in this book.

My friends and colleagues in the magical arts are long gone before me, and I am old. Merlin, Flamel, Agrippa...their names are known to the world. But I have chosen to remain in the shadows, to hone my craft and exercise my powers for the good of mankind. Now I am ready to rest.

Once upon a time when I was young like you—

AS MY LEGACY, I LEAVE YOU THIS BOOK. USE IT WELL.

and everyone looks young to me now— I began to learn the wizardly arts.

In the year 1400, the world was a dark place. Ignorance and brute force ruled, while a few of us kept the bright stars of learning, hope, and wonder alive.

Out of necessity, our schools were kept secret. Too many intolerant and fearful people were lighting bonfires to burn the visionary, the gifted, and the different. For the past 600 years, I have kept notes, recipes, fabulous tales, and discoveries in this secret book

of mine, thinking someday I would bequeath it to the deserving.

So young wizards, are you ready to inherit my knowledge, and to learn how to become what I was? Are your shoulders strong enough to wear the wizard's robe and your hands agile enough to wield the magic wand? If you are ready, this book will tell you how to create all these things with ease, and how to use them, because a good wizard knows many arts.

Most important, practice the art of making other people laugh. Be sure to laugh at yourself, too, because a great wizard has a great sense of humor. Think how dull life would be if we were serious all the time, for goodness' sake! A wink here and a joke there has helped me live to a great old age, and I've enjoyed every minute of my 600-plus years.

You will never know my name. It is better that way. But the next time something happens that seems mysterious, magical, or beautiful, think of me. And give credit to your own powers to make the wonderful happen.

THE DAY I PUT ON MY FIRST ROBE
WAS THE HAPPIEST DAY OF MY LIFE.

Chapter I

WIZARD REGALIA

It's said that clothes make the man or woman, and that definitely includes wizards. Here are my notes on how to make some of my favorite robes, hats, slippers, and special adornments. Read on to find out how to make magic wands and staffs, wizard money, and a high-speed broom for when you need to get somewhere fast! To hold all your new wizard gear, I also include the design for my Wizard's Trunk. I went through quite a few of those in my travels around the world through the ages. (I recall I threw my last trunk at a giant squid that was trying to swamp my ship in the Pacific Ocean. By the time the monster decided which of its arms to use to catch it, I'd made my escape.)

Sorcerer's Hat

You can almost create this hat out of thin air—it's that easy. You don't need much material, and, as if by magic, the hat practically sews itself! Any color you like will work fine, (although my great aunt Cecilia believed that only red was powerful enough for a proper hat).

Or use the color of your astrological sign. I'm a Pisces, and my color is purple. To discover your astrological color, see pages 105 to 107.

Or use the color of your astrological sign. I'm a Pisces, and my color is purple. To discover your astrological color, see pages 105 to 107.

WHAT YOU NEED

- ½ yard (45 cm) fabric or felt
- ½ yard (45 cm) fusible interfacing (the stiffest kind)
- ¾-yard-wide (69 cm) wire-edge ribbon
- measuring tape
- pencil
- calculator (unless you are especially adept in arithmancy skills)
- sheet of newspaper
- ruler
- scissors
- straight pins
- fabric glue
- sewing machine or needle and thread*
- iron

For decoration (choose one or all):
- fabric scraps
- wide ribbon or braid
- metallic-colored acrylic paints
- paintbrush
- glitter
- rubber stamps

*Note: You don't have to sew this hat if you make it out of felt or paper. Simply use glue or an iron-on fabric adhesive to make the seam.

INSTRUCTIONS

1. Measure the circumference of your head right above the ears with a measuring tape. Multiply that measurement by 4; then, divide that number by 6.28. (And some of you still wonder why it's so important to learn math!)

2. Measure and mark a line as long as what you came up with in step 1 (on the top edge of the sheet of newspaper). Measure and mark a second line at a right angle to the first line. Use a ruler or measuring tape to mark equal points from the right angle. Connect the points with a line forming an arc. See figure 1.

3. Use scissors to cut out the quarter-circle you just drew (figure 1).

4. Place the pattern on your fabric. Pin the pattern to the fabric, and add a 1/2-inch (1.3 cm) seam allowance to the straight edges of the pattern. Cut out the pattern.

5. If you wish to decorate your hat, do so before seaming it. Work on a flat surface. Decorate the fabric with stars, crescent moons, alchemical, or astrological symbols. You can paint them freehand, or you can trace the alchemical symbols on page 141. Metallic-colored acrylic paints used with rubber stamps, or metallic gel marking pens work, too. Or cut out shapes from gold or silver scraps of fabric, and glue them to the cutout hat. See figure 2.

6. Lay the decorated fabric on the fusible interfacing. Cut around the fabric. Follow the manufacturer's instructions included with the interfacing that explains how to use an iron to fuse it to the fabric (figure 2).

7. Match the straight sides, right sides together. Sew a 1/2-inch (1.3 cm) seam along this edge by hand or with a sewing machine.

8. Turn the hat right sides out.

9. You can decorate the rim of the hat by stitching or gluing on a decorative ribbon or braid. If you want a dressier look, gather one end of a piece of wire-edge ribbon and stitch it to the back of the hat. Gather the ribbon about 3 inches (7.5 cm) from this end, stitch it to the hat, and repeat as many times as needed around the rim of the hat (figure 3).

WHO, WHOO, WHOOOOO Goes There?

Picking the Right Owl for Wizard Work

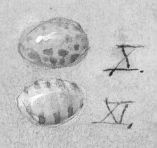

What do you think of when you picture an owl? Its huge eyes, probably. Some people think the owl's eyes make it look kind and wise, while others think they're scary. But did you know that if humans had eyes in the same proportion to the size of their heads as a great horned owl, our eyes would be the size of grapefruit and weigh five pounds (2.3 kg) each? Now, that's scary!

My friend Merlin rarely went anywhere without his owl Archimedes, and if you think about how owls are built and what they do, you can imagine how they can be helpful to a wizard. Owls can see in the dark, they can hear very faint noises, and they're great at grabbing and carrying things.

Owls are perfectly built for hunting at night and in twilight. The Greeks actually thought owls carried a magic light inside their eyes that helped them see at night! Their eyes are four times more sensitive to light than humans'. They have a wide angle of vision, but their eyes are fixed in their sockets so the owl has to turn its entire head to look sideways. To make up for that, owls' necks are so flexible they can turn their heads 270 degrees to look backward over their shoulders, or they can

turn their heads upside down! They have very large ear holes, and one ear is higher on their head than the other one, allowing owls to locate the distance and direction of very faint noises.

Owls can fly in complete silence because their feathers are constructed with special down and fringed edges that eliminate the sound of air rushing over them. Their feet have very large, piercing talons with an opposable back toe, similar to how the human thumb works. An owl's beak doesn't look very large, but that's because feathers cover a lot of it. When they open their beak wide, most owls can swallow small mammals whole.

The eagle owl (*Bubo bubo*), also called the Eurasian eagle owl, is the largest species of owl. It measures up to 2 feet, 4 inches (71.1 cm) and weighs up to 8 pounds (3.6 kg). The owl has big orange eyes, and it's called a horned owl because it has two feather tufts on its head. It roosts in rocky overhangs and hollow trees. The eagle owl has been seen carrying grown foxes in its talons, and is known to go after animals the size of a small deer!

On the other hand, the elf owl (*Micrathene whitney*) is tinier than most mammals. Five inches (12.7 cm) long, it weighs only 1-1/2 ounces (42 g), and is the world's smallest owl. It has a

rounded head, yellow eyes, and white eyebrows. Elf owls like to live in the desert, and they're so tiny, they nest in woodpecker holes! They have a high-pitched, squeaky call.

Nearer the middle in terms of size, you'll find the barn owl. It has a round head with a heart-shaped, white face, and a mottled rust-gray body. Found almost everywhere around the world, it measures 15 to 18 inches (38.1 to 45.7 cm) long and weighs up to a pound (454 g). The barn owl lives in rural areas, man-made constructions such as bridges, and natural locations such as hollow trees. Its call sounds more like a series of two-second screeches. If you have a problem with mice or rats in your castle, you can solve it with barn owls, because one barn owl family can eat 1,200 rats a month.

Our beliefs about owls reflect both our fear and admiration of them. The Greeks believed the owl could prophesy the future, and the Little Owl (*Athene noctua*) was the symbol of Athena, the Greek goddess of wisdom. If an owl flew over Greek soldiers before a battle, it was an omen they would win. But to the Romans, if an owl hooted while a person was in their sickbed, death was not far away. Owls predicted the deaths of the Roman emperor Julius Caesar and the famous magician Agrippa.

Feather & Jewel Turban

A wrapping of gold, one dazzling jewel,
a needle and thread, some fabric glue.
Create your own turban, it's simple to do.
Feather of owl or cockatoo—I'll leave that to you.

WHAT YOU NEED

- measuring tape
- pencil and paper
- newspaper
- ruler
- $1/2$ yard (46 cm) fabric of your choice
- straight pins
- scissors
- iron
- fusible hem tape or fabric glue
- sewing needle and thread (that matches fabric)
- sewing machine (optional)
- costume jewelry pin
- large feather
- small cardboard circle covered with aluminum foil (optional)
- colored markers (optional)

INSTRUCTIONS

1. Ask a friend to measure around your head—right above your ears—with a measuring tape. Write the measurement down on a piece of paper. Add $1^{1}/2$ inches (3.8 cm) to this measurement.

2. Measure and mark the total measurement in step 1 on the edge of a sheet of newspaper.

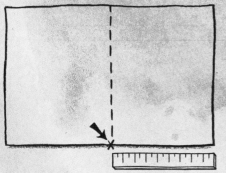

FIGURE 1

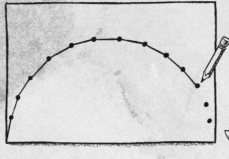

FIGURE 2

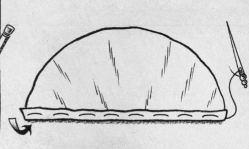

FIGURE 3

3. Divide the line in half and mark the line at the center point (see figure 1). If the center point is 12 inches (30.5 cm), use the ruler to mark an arc from this center point in several places. Connect these marks with a pencil line to make a semicircle (see figure 2). This is the pattern for your turban.

4. Place your fabric on a table. Smooth out any wrinkles with your hands. Lay your newspaper pattern on top of the fabric. Use straight pins to pin it to the fabric. Carefully cut out the pattern and the fabric.

5. Place your fabric right side down and fold up a $1/2$-inch (1.3 cm) hem on the long, straight line of the fabric (see figure 3). Press this hem with your fingers or a hot iron. Use fusible hem tape, fabric glue, or a needle and thread to finish the hem.

6. Fold the semicircle in half, right sides together (see figure 4). Pin the fabric together in two places. This will make sewing easier. Thread a

needle with a double length of thread, and knot the thread at the end. Sew about $1/4$ inch (6 mm) in from the curved edge. Try to make your stitches about $1/2$ inch (1.3 cm) long.

7. Gather the curved edge by pushing the fabric towards the knotted end of the thread while holding the needle end of the thread (see figure 5). Work slowly and carefully so you don't break the thread. When you have gathered the curved edge, finish with a few stitches to hold the end of the thread. Cut off the end of the thread. Turn the turban right side out.

FIGURE 4

8. On the front of the turban where you have fastened it with stitches, attach the costume jewelry pin. Behind the pin, slide in the feather. If you don't have a fancy pin, cut out a circle from a piece of cardboard, as large as you wish your decoration to be. Cover it with aluminum foil. You may color the foil with markers, if you wish. Then, thread a needle with a length of thread, knot it at the end, and sew it to the front of the turban as you would a button.

FIGURE 5

Wizard's Robe

This is THE essential garment—if you are truly serious about your craft. This robe is very easy to make, even if you have never sewn anything before. You can sew it by hand or with a sewing machine. Making your own robe also gives you the opportunity to practice basic math skills—something of utmost importance for every young wizard and sorceress. Choose wisely the color you want for your robe. Certain colors, such as dark blue, symbolize impulsiveness and changeability, which may destabilize certain spells, if you are in a distracted mood. Light blue, conversely, represents patience and tranquility. Purple, a favorite color of mine, symbolizes ambition and power, but if you are feeling frivolous, it may attract the attention of troublesome trolls.

WHAT YOU NEED

- measuring tape
- fabric yardage (see step 1)
- pencil, chalk, or other fabric marker
- straight pins
- scissors
- sewing needle and thread to match fabric
- sewing machine (optional)
- fusible hem tape or fabric glue (optional)
- bias tape
- 18 inches (46 cm) heavy cording
- photocopies of symbols on page 141
- tracing paper
- water-soluble pen (optional)
- dress-maker's carbon paper (optional)
- large piece of cardboard
- fabric paint in colors of your choice
- paintbrush
- fusible webbing
- iron
- decorative trim, cording, or printed ribbon

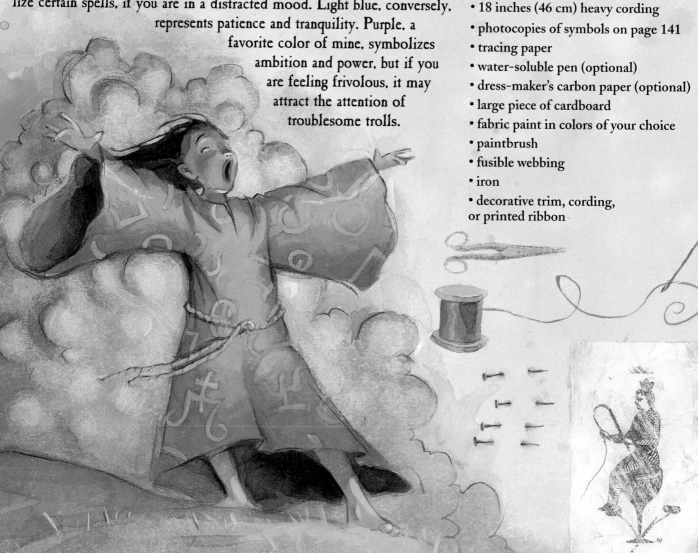

INSTRUCTIONS

Making the Robe

1. Ask a fellow wizard or sorceress to measure you with the tape measure so that you can determine how much fabric you will need. Stand with your arms down by your sides. Have your friend measure you from the top of your shoulder to the floor; then add 1 inch (2.5 cm) for the hem. Multiply this measurement by 2 to determine the cut length of fabric needed. Now have your friend measure you from one wrist to the other, across the back of your shoulders, and then add 2 inches (5 cm) for the sleeve hems. This measurement will determine the width of the fabric you will need.

Fabrics 45 inches (114 cm) wide are usually wide enough for most wizards under the age of 10. Older wizards (or those with long arms) will require wider fabrics or will need to sew on extra fabric for the sleeves.

Now measure loosely around the base of the neck. Lastly, measure your inside arm length (from wrist to underarm), minus 2 inches (5 cm). Write all these measurements down for future reference.

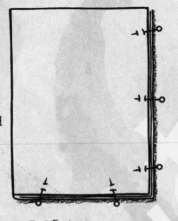

FIGURE 1

2. Fold the length of fabric in half, right sides together. Lay the folded fabric flat on a large tabletop or the floor, smoothing out the wrinkles as you work. Pin the bottom edges together in several places.

3. Fold the fabric in half lengthwise (you will have four layers of fabric). Secure the open edges with a few straight pins.
See figure 1.

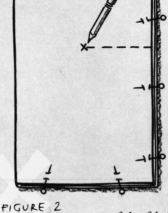

FIGURE 2

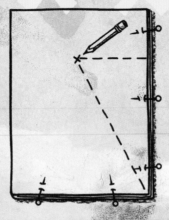

FIGURE 3

4. Divide the total measurement from wrist to wrist, including the hem allowance, by 2. This measurement is the sleeve length. Measure and mark from the folded edge of the fabric to the sleeve length.

5. Determine how wide you wish the sleeve of the gown to be; 12 to 15 inches (30.5 to 38 cm) wide should be fine. Make a parallel mark on the unfolded open side with a pencil or chalk to the chosen measurement. From this mark, draw a line equal to the inside arm length running parallel to the top fold.
See figure 2.

6. Draw a line from the open edge at the bottom of the fabric to the mark for the inside arm length. See figure 3.

7. For the neckline, divide the neck measurement by 6. Measure and mark a point on the top and side folds from the folded corner. Connect the marks with a curved line to form an arc. See figure 4.

8. Cut through all the layers for the neckline and along the lines marked for the sleeve and sides. See figure 5.

9. Open up the robe and lay it flat. It will look like a T-shape, with the fold at the top.

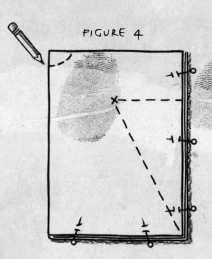

FIGURE 4

10. Sew the side and sleeve seams with a $\frac{1}{2}$-inch (1.3 cm) seam allowance, by hand or by machine. Turn the robe right side out.

11. You can use fusible hem tape or fabric glue, if you do not wish to sew the hems of the sleeves and the bottom of the robe.

12. Cut a 4-inch (10.2 cm) slit from the neckline down the center front of the robe. See figure 6.

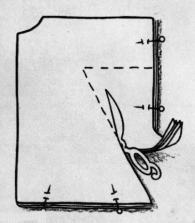

FIGURE 5

13. To finish the edges, attach bias tape by machine or hand.

14. Use the heavy cording as a belt for the robe.

FIGURE 6

Decorating the Robe

1. First you will need to transfer the alchemical symbols onto the fabric (the symbols are on page 141). There are several ways to do this:

• Tracing: The easiest way is to trace the symbols onto the fabric using a water-soluable pen or very sharp pencil. Simply draw or trace the symbols onto a piece of tracing paper and tape it to a window. Then tape the fabric on top and trace the pattern onto it.

• Dressmaker's carbon paper: This special fabric carbon comes in different colors so that you can select one that will clearly show on your fabric. Draw, trace, or photocopy the pattern. Place the fabric on a clean, flat surface and tape it down with masking tape. Place the carbon paper face down on top and tape it down. Use a ballpoint pen to trace carefully over the pattern.

2. Use fabric paint to paint the symbols. (Of course, you can choose other designs—this is your robe.) Be sure to place the cardboard inside the robe before you paint on the fabric, or the paint will seep through both layers. Paint the neckline, sleeve, and bottom of the robe hems with strips or swirls of paint that look good with the painted-on symbols. Read the manufacturer's instructions that come with the fabric paint to find out how to heat-set the colors using a hot iron. Ask an adult for help with this!

3. Enlarge the patterns on a copy machine. Use these patterns to cut out shapes from contrasting colors and textures of fabric. Attach the fabric shapes to the robe with fusible webbing.

4. Attach decorative trim, cording, or printed ribbon to the hem edges of the sleeves, neck, and bottom. You can do this either by stitching the trim in place or with fusible hem tape or fabric glue.

Hourglass Pendant

No wizard or sorceress should be without this simple pendant. It's very useful for timing the simmering of potions.

WHAT YOU NEED

- 3-minute kitchen timer*
- 48 inches (1.2 m) of sturdy cord
- scissors

*sold for just a few bronze coins at kitchen-supply stores

INSTRUCTIONS

1. Fold the cord in half and cut at the fold.

2. Lay one piece of the cord flat on a work surface.

3. Find the center of the cord, and lay your timer on it so that the small center section of the timer crosses the cord.

4. Lay the other piece of cord on top of the timer.

5. Use the top and bottom cords to tie a simple knot on each side of the timer. This will secure the timer on the cord.

6. Hold the pendant around your neck and decide where you want the timer to hang on your chest. Knot the cords together and trim the excess.

Wand with Dragon Heartstrings

Coils of dragon heartstrings make a pleasant sound that only fairies can hear when you cast spells with this wand.

WHAT YOU NEED

- spool of brass or copper wire*
- ruler
- wire cutters
- pencil
- 2-inch (5 cm) polystyrene foam ball*
- gold or silver glitter
- white craft glue
- disposable plate or meat tray
- disposable paintbrush
- straight twig or wooden dowel, about 18 inches (45.7 cm) long and $\frac{1}{2}$ inch (1.3 cm) wide
- acrylic paint (gold or silver)
- paintbrush
- hot glue gun and glue sticks

*sold in craft stores

INSTRUCTIONS

1. Measure and cut eight lengths of wire, each 18 inches (45.7 cm) long.

2. Tightly wind the wire around a pencil. Leave about 2 inches (5 cm) unwound (see figure 1 on page 20). Repeat this process with the other seven lengths of wire.

3. Lightly press the polystyrene foam ball onto the end of the stick so that it sinks down about 1 inch (2.5 cm) onto the stick.

4. Pour gold or silver glitter onto the plate. Using the disposable paintbrush, coat the ball with the white glue. Then, roll it in the glitter to coat it well. (see figure 2). Allow it to dry.

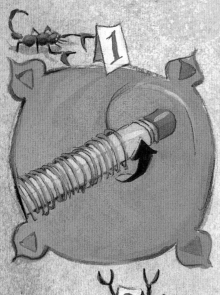

5. Use a clean paintbrush to paint the twig or dowel with gold or silver acrylic paint. Allow it to dry.

6. Use hot glue to attach the ball to the wand.

7. Put a dot of hot glue on the straight end of a wire coil, and insert the end into the foam ball (see figure 3). Repeat with the rest of the coils.

8. Make additional coils and insert them into the ball if desired.

Sorceress Wand

Like a maypole in spring
Like butterfly wings
Ribbons of bright color
Set gentle spells a-flutter.

WHAT YOU NEED

• **4 yards (3.7 m) of ¼ inch-wide (6 mm) ribbon in different colors**
• **measuring tape**
• **scissors**
• **straight twig or wooden dowel, about 18 inches (45.7 cm) long and ½ inch (1.3 cm) wide**
• **acrylic paint (gold or silver)**
• **paintbrush**
• **hot glue gun and glue sticks**
• **decorative upholstery tack**
• **small hammer**

INSTRUCTIONS

1. Measure and cut four lengths of ribbon, each 18 inches (45.7 cm) long, and one length of ribbon 24 inches (61 cm) long. Set them aside.

2. Paint the wand with gold or silver acrylic paint, and allow it to dry.

3. Use hot glue to attach one end of the long ribbon to one end of the wand. Wind the ribbon up the wand, gluing it in place every 2 inches (5 cm). Cut off the excess ribbon, and glue the tip of the ribbon to the other end of the wand.

4. Center the four lengths of ribbon on the tip of the wand in a spoke-like fashion. Glue each ribbon to the tip with a small dot of hot glue. Then, use a hammer to fix an upholstery tack to the tip of the wand, fastening the ribbons securely.

GREAT WIZARDS
I Have Known

One of the best things about being a wizard has been the people I have known over the past several hundred years, especially my friends in the magical arts. They were all memorable, especially Agrippa and his mysterious black dog, and Merlin, even if he was terribly untidy at times, with all those mice and birds living in his hair and beard. Cherish your friends, I say—they'll be gone some day.

Just about every village in Britain and Europe used to have its own wizard who told fortunes, found lost objects and treasure, interpreted dreams, made love potions, and drove away troublesome fairies. These days, wizards are more hidden, but they can still be found.

Circe was a powerful Greek sorceress who, according to the poet Homer, controlled fate by braiding knots in her hair. I thought she had a great sense of humor, myself. As Homer told the story, Circe was quite enchanting, and lured the wandering hero Odysseus and his sailors onto her island. What did she do then? Turned the men into pigs! Odysseus made her change them back into men, but he was so taken with her, he dallied there for a year.

Whether you know him as Merlinus, Myrddin, or Merlin, you know who I'm talking about. He was one of our greatest wizards, and the most famous. Some stories say Merlin was a Druid, and that he was born in Wales to a royal princess and a supernatural father. Though he could have

chosen evil, Merlin decided to use his supernatural abilities only for good. He could see the future, cast spells, and perform wonderful acts of magic. Merlin was a prophet and advisor to several British rulers including King Arthur. It's said that Merlin helped erect Stonehenge and used magic to bring together Arthur's parents, Uther and Igraine, so that Arthur would be born to them. Merlin tutored the young Arthur, and arranged for him to pull the famous sword from a stone, which legend said would remain embedded until it was removed by a man virtuous enough to be king. Merlin was also behind the idea of the Round Table, and his advice helped Arthur to govern Camelot and defend his kingdom against invading Saxons.

It's said that Merlin went with Arthur to the magical Isle of Avalon after Arthur was wounded in his final battle. Others believe that Merlin's downfall came when he fell in love with Nimue, who persuaded Merlin to teach her all his arts and then imprisoned him in a hawthorn tree. But do you really believe a wizard as powerful as Merlin would remain trapped forever? Some say that Merlin waits in a crystal cave, guarding the True Throne of the realm, where Arthur will sit again one day.

Did you know the word wizard comes from the Middle English word WIS, meaning wise?

Morgan le Fay was either Arthur's sister or half-sister, I was never sure. She had many magical powers, but she had a reputation for constantly trying to lure handsome knights into her chambers. Even Merlin fell under her spell for awhile. She wasn't all bad, though. Morgan was gifted at healing with herbs, and when Arthur was wounded in his last battle, she helped get him safely to Avalon and used her powers to save his life.

Agrippa was the most famous magician of the Renaissance and served in the courts of five kings. His full name was Heinrich Cornelius Agrippa von Nettesheim, and he wrote a very popular, three-volume book about magic. Agrippa was also a doctor, a diplomat, and a war hero, but when he championed causes for social justice such as land reform for peasants, he was thrown out of several different countries. Agrippa was frequently poor and paid innkeepers with money that later turned into seashells. Legend says that Agrippa always travelled with a mysterious black dog that wore a collar engraved with magic symbols. As the magician lay dying, he took the collar off the dog and commanded the animal to depart. The dog ran away, dove into a river, and was never seen again.

Magic Amulet

This clay amulet is designed for directing magical energy. Before you put it around your neck, hold it between both your hands, close your eyes, and repeat the following incantation:

Round my neck a circle goes
Guiding my magic as it grows.
By all the might of moon and sun
As I do will, it shall be done.

WHAT YOU NEED

• 2-ounce (56 g) block of white or light-colored polymer clay
• table knife
• resealable sandwich bag
• rolling pin or straight-sided jar for flattening the clay
• photocopy of scarab beetle design
• scissors
• metal spoon
• knitting needle or chopstick
• cookie sheet covered with aluminum foil
• oven

• hot pads
• colored pencils (optional)
• black pencil
• 18 inches (45.7 cm) of cord in silk, rayon, leather, or hemp

INSTRUCTIONS

1. Use the table knife to cut the 2-ounce (56 g) block of polymer clay in half. Place one half in the resealable sandwich bag and set it aside.

2. Knead the clay in your hands. Roll it into a ball, then stretch it out. Repeat this action several times until the clay is soft and warm.

3. Roll the clay into a ball in your hands. Put it on a smooth, clean work surface and flatten it out with the palm of your hand. Use the rolling pin or a straight-sided jar to roll out the clay until it is about $1/8$ inch (3 mm) thick.

4. Make a photocopy of the scarab design. You can make the image larger or smaller, if necessary. Keep in mind that the transferred image will be a mirror image of the original. The toner used in copy machines is what will transfer to the clay; inkjet printer ink will not work. Use your photocopied image right away to make sure the transfer works well.

5. Cut out your photocopied scarab. You will need to shape and trim the clay so that the design will look good on it. Use the table knife to cut the clay to the correct shape and size.

6. Place the photocopied scarab face down on the clay. To transfer the design onto the clay, gently rub the back of the paper with the spoon. Don't rub too hard or you will change the shape. Let the clay and paper sit for 10 minutes.

7. Use the tip of the knitting needle or chopstick to make one or two holes in the clay through which later you will thread your cord.

8. Gently and carefully move your clay to the cookie sheet.

9. Preheat the oven according to the manufacturer's instructions on the package of polymer clay. When the oven is ready, put the cookie sheet in the oven. Be sure you leave the paper on the clay!

10. Bake the clay for 10 to 15 minutes. Use the hot pads to remove the cookie sheet from the oven. While the clay is still warm, carefully remove the paper to reveal your transferred image. Let the clay sit until it is completely cool.

11. If you want to color the clay with the colored pencils, now is the time to do it. Use several layers of color to darken the color. Use the black pencil to darken the lines from the photocopy transfer.

12. To complete the amulet you need to use a little knot magic. Measure and cut a piece of cord so the amulet will hang around your neck to the desired length. If you made one hole in the amulet, double the cord and thread the fold through the hole. Then, pass the free ends through the loop and pull it tight. Knot the two free ends. If you made two holes in the amulet, make a double or triple knot at one end of the cord. Thread the unknotted end through one hole, pull the knot to the amulet, and then thread through the opposite hole and knot that end as well. As you tie each knot, imagine it is holding positive, healing energy which is released when you wear the amulet.

THE SCARAB BEETLE WAS A MYSTICAL CREATURE AND A VERY POWERFUL SYMBOL TO THE ANCIENT EGYPTIANS.

The NOW YOU SEE ME, now you don't Cloak

The magic power of this cloak is strengthened when the fabric is lightweight, the color shimmery, and the texture like silk. Think butterfly wings. Cumulus cloud. Shadow on the wall. Waterfall. Imagine yourself disappearing and reappearing silently.

WHAT YOU NEED

- measuring tape
- fabric of your choice (see step 1)
- straight pins
- calculator
- pencil or chalk
- ruler
- scissors
- matching thread
- sewing needle or sewing machine
- 1 yard (.9 m) of decorative ribbon

Optional Materials for Decoration

- fabric scraps for decorative appliqués
- fusible hem tape and webbing
- fabric paints
- rubber stamps

INSTRUCTIONS

Making the Cloak

1. Decide how long you want your cloak. Use a measuring tape to measure from the base of your neck across your shoulders. Then measure from your shoulder to your ankles. You will need to buy enough fabric to make a square the same dimension as this measurement. The cloak itself is made from a circle cut from a folded square of fabric. For example, if you need a cloak 36 inches (.9 m) long, you will need to buy 2 yards (1.8 m) of fabric at least 72 inches (1.8 m) wide. If necessary, you can sew together two widths of yardage. Purchase an extra 1/2 yard (45.7 cm) of the fabric for the hood.

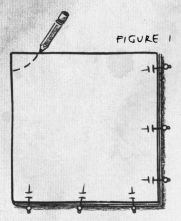

FIGURE 1

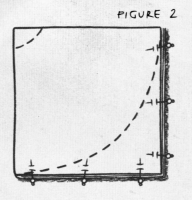

FIGURE 2

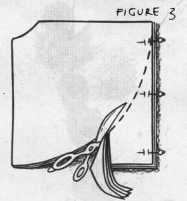

FIGURE 3

2. Fold the square of fabric in half lengthwise, then crosswise. Use straight pins to pin the four layers together.

3. Use a measuring tape to measure around the base of the neck. Use a calculator to divide this measure-

ment by 3.14; then divide the result by 2. This will give you the correct measurement to create the neckline. Mark an arc on the fabric from the folded center using a ruler and pencil or chalk (see figure 1).

4. Mark an arc for the bottom edge of the cloak, measuring from the center fold a distance equal to the length of the cape (see figure 2).

5. Cut on the marked lines through all layers. (See figure 3). Cut one of the folded edges for the center front opening

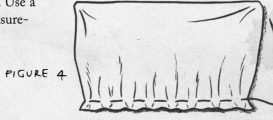

FIGURE 4

Making the Hood

1. Measure from the base of your neck to the top of your head. Add 6 inches (15 cm) to this measurement. This will determine the height of your hood. Mark a rectangle on the fabric, using the neck to the top of head measurement and the measurement around the base of the neck, plus 6 inches as the two sides of the rectangle.

FIGURE 5

2. On the long side of the rectangle, sew a straight line of $1/2$-inch (1.3 cm) stitches about $1/2$ inch from the edge. Use this line of stitching to gather the edge of the rectangle to fit the neckline (see figure 4). Pin together the right sides of the gathered edge and the cape neckline. Stitch the two layers together with a $1/2$-inch seam by hand or machine. Finish the raw edge by trimming close to the seam.

3. Turn the attached hood right sides together. Match the free corners, and use straight pins to pin the top edges together (see figure 5). Stitch together using a $1/2$-inch (1.3 cm) seam. Trim the raw edges close to the seam.

4. Hem the bottom edge and opening edges of the cape and hood, if desired.

5. Cut the ribbon into two equal lengths. Use a needle and thread to stitch a length to each side at the neck opening.

6. Decorate the cloak as desired.

TALES OF THE
CELTIC Shape-shifters

To the ancient Celts, there weren't distinct boundaries separating the Celtic gods, people, and animals. They believed their gods could shape shift, to change into human or animal form, that there were people with supernatural powers who could change into animals, and that enchanted animals existed which were once human. The most famous myths are full of shape-shifters.

Celtic legend says that the goddess Cerridwen gave birth both to the wizard Merlin and to the great sixth-century Celtic bard, or poet, named Taliesin. Cerridwen was the goddess of wisdom, magic, and divination. Here is the story of how she became Taliesin's birth mother.

Long ago, Cerridwen had a son named Morfran the Dark. Some people said he was ugly and without talent. To help her son, Cerridwen created a magic cauldron. She put herbs, roots, and sacred water in the vessel to simmer for a year and a day, planning to use the brew to pass on all her knowledge to her son. She put a young boy named Gwion in charge of stirring the cauldron. When the brew was finished, Morfran would taste three drops and he would receive all of Cerridwen's knowledge and power. But Gwion did not let this happen. The night before the official tasting, Gwion stuck his thumb into the hot cauldron and sucked on his finger to cool it, drinking three drops of the magic mixture. The cauldron shook and cracked, waking up Cerridwen.

Realizing what had happened, Cerridwen chased the thief. Gwion used his new powers to change into a hare and run away. Cerridwen shape-shifted into a greyhound and almost caught him, but Gwion turned into a fish and dove into a river. Cerridwen changed into an otter, but once again, just before she caught the fish, Gwion changed into a bird and flew into the sky. The goddess changed into a giant hawk, ready to fall on the smaller bird. But Gwion saw wheat in a field below, and changed himself into a tiny grain to hide. Cerridwen spotted him, changed into a hen, and pecked at the grain, eating Gwion.

But the tiny grain of wheat that was Gwion grew into a baby over the next nine months. Cerridwen realized she couldn't bring herself to kill the newborn child, but instead tied Gwion in a leather sack and threw him in a river. Legend says that someone fished the sack from the river on All Hallow's Eve (called Samhain by the Celts) and that the reborn Gwion became the Celts' greatest poet and storyteller, Taliesin.

Fingerless Gloves

Chant a spell
Only time will tell
Slip on this pair
Wave your wand in the air.

Gloves like this bring magic close.
Be careful what you wish for most!

WHAT YOU NEED

• **pair of old cotton gloves**
• **pencil**
• **scissors**

INSTRUCTIONS

1. Slip on the gloves. Use the pencil to mark where you want the fingers and thumb of the gloves to be trimmed off. Remove the gloves.

2. Place the gloves on your work surface, and carefully cut off the fingers and thumbs where you marked.

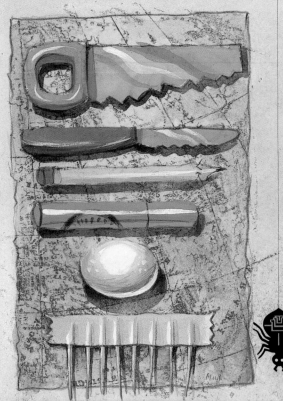

Wizard's Staffs

I have quite a collection of staffs—
252 of them, to be exact. My wife was a very
good sport about the clutter, but she never got used to the
Anubis-headed staff because of its habit of howling at every
full moon. (According to the ancient Egyptians, Anubis was
a powerful god with a jackal's head.)With simple paper mache,
you can make a staff like that one, although there's no telling
if yours will be a howler. Or you can make the basic staff,
and decorate it with animal designs that are meaningful to you.

WHAT YOU NEED
(FOR THE BASIC STAFF)

• wooden closet rod, broomstick,
large fallen branch from a tree (don't
cut a branch, use one that has fallen)
• measuring tape
• pencil
• handsaw
• 8 feet (2.5 m) of small
diameter rope*
• hot glue gun and glue sticks
• acrylic paint in color of your choice
• paintbrush
• craft knife or scissors

*Wander down the aisles of your local
hardware/home improvement store; this is
where modern-day wizards can find many
of their supplies.

INSTRUCTIONS

1. The length of a wizard's staff
should be in proportion to the wizard for whom it is made. A good
rule of thumb is to make the staff 6
inches (15 cm) shorter than the wizard or sorceress. Measure and mark
the staff material you have chosen.

2. Use a handsaw to cut off any
extra length.

3. Use hot glue to attach one end of
the rope to the bottom of the staff.

4. Wind the rope up the staff at an
angle, gluing the rope to the staff
about every 2 inches (5 cm).
(See figure 1 on page 30). When you
are about 2 inches (5 cm) from the

other end of the staff, stop winding
and gluing. Make sure you have
about 10 inches (25 cm) of loose
rope left.

5. Paint the staff, including the rope,
and allow it to dry. Do not paint the
last 2 inches (5 cm) at the top of the
staff.

6. Use hot glue to attach the ornament to the top of the staff. Wind
and glue the last bit of rope around
the bottom of the staff ornament. If
necessary, cut off the excess rope.
Touch up this section of the staff
with paint.

WHAT YOU NEED
(FOR THE ANUBIS HEAD)

- Anubis Head template on page 31
- pencil
- scissors
- black marker
- 1 block of floral foam*
- table knife
- polystyrene foam egg*
- hot glue gun and glue stick*
- toothpicks
- newspaper or tissue paper
- plastic sheeting
- white craft glue
- small bowl
- plastic wrap
- gesso or acrylic primer*
- acrylic paint in gold or other colors
- paintbrushes

*sold in craft stores

INSTRUCTIONS

1. Photocopy and enlarge the side view template of the Anubis head, and cut it out. Place the head template on the floral foam block, and trace around it with the marker.

2. Position the head on the top of the staff and gently push the block about 1 inch (2.5 cm) onto the staff.

3. Remove the foam block. Set the block down on a table with the traced shape facing up. Use a table knife and a sawing motion to cut away the foam around the shape you have traced on the block. (SEE FIGURE 2 ON PAGE 30.)

Then, use the knife to round the sharp edges of the head shape and to narrow the snout end.

29

5. Tear newspaper or tissue paper into 1/2-inch (1.3 cm) strips. If you want evenly torn strips, tear the paper by pulling a strip against a ruler held down on the paper. You'll need a couple of good handfuls of strips. Set the strips aside.

6. Make a mixture of three parts white glue and one part water in a small bowl. Stir the mixture to an even consistency.

4. Use the knife to cut the foam egg in half lengthwise (figure 3). Cut one half in half lengthwise again. These skinny slices will form the ears. Insert a toothpick in the rounded end of each ear. Put the ears in position on the head. You may wish to trim the sharp edges further with a knife. Secure the toothpicks in the ears with hot glue, and secure the ears to the head with hot glue.

9. Begin applying strips to the head form, overlapping the strips as you cover it (figure 4). Cover the form with one layer of strips, smoothing the strips as you work; then set the head aside to dry. Cover your bowl with plastic wrap to prevent the glue mixture from drying out.

7. Cover your working area with plastic sheeting or newspaper. This is messy work, but I quite like it.

8. Dip one strip of paper at a time in the bowl. Run the paper between your thumb and forefinger to wring excess liquid from the strip.

10. Put at least three layers of paper strips on the form. Allow each layer to dry overnight before adding the next layer. The head form will be smoother and stronger with additional layers.

11. When the final layer is dry, brush a coat of gesso or acrylic primer on the head, and let it dry.

12. Paint the head gold or another color that matches the staff. Allow it to dry.

13. Use a pencil to draw the eye of Horus, the ancient Egyptian Sky God, on the head. Use a dark color to paint the eye, as shown in figure 5. Allow it to dry.

14. Use a generous amount of hot glue to attach the head to the top of the staff.

ENLARGE THIS ANUBIS HEAD TEMPLATE 145% SO IT IS ABOUT 10 INCHES (25 CM) LONG.

JEWELED ORB
SHOWN ON PAGE 29

WHAT YOU NEED
(FOR THE JEWELED ORB)

- 6-inch (15 cm) polystyrene foam ball*
- table knife
- newspaper to cover work surface
- disposable plate or foam meat tray
- glitter
- white craft glue
- disposable paintbrush
- hot glue gun and glue sticks
- large plastic gems in a variety of shapes and colors
- basic staff (page 28)

*sold in craft stores

INSTRUCTIONS

1. Center the polystyrene foam ball on the staff and gently push on it to make an indentation in the ball; then remove the ball. Use the table knife to hollow out a hole 1 inch (2.5 cm) deep and slightly smaller than the indentation.

2. Pour glitter on the disposable plate.

3. Paint the foam ball with a thin coat of white craft glue. Roll it in the glitter, and allow it to dry for a few minutes.

4. Use hot glue to attach the jewels to the ball.

5. Fill the hole with hot glue, and gently push the ball onto the basic staff.

Wizard Reticule and Coins

Wizards and sorceresses never go anywhere without a handy reticule tied to the belt of their robe. This leather pouch is perfect for holding wizard coins, magical herbs, or a divining ring. Wizard coins can be any shape: square, rectangular, oval, or triangular. Have plenty of silver magical moola on hand — the price of dragon eggs these days is outrageous!

WHAT YOU NEED
(FOR THE RETICULE)

• piece of chamois, about 18 inches (45.7 cm) square*
(optional fabrics include any type of cloth, felt, or scrap leather)

• circular template (dinner plate, bucket, or large lid of plastic food container)
• pencil
• scissors
• paper punch or large, sharp nail
• 1 yard (.9 m) twine, heavy string, or leather thong

*found in auto-supply stores

MAKE YOUR RETICULE LARGE ENOUGH TO HOLD A KING'S RANSOM IN WIZARD COINS.

INSTRUCTIONS
(FOR THE RETICULE)

1. Smooth out the chamois cloth on a tabletop. Use a pencil to trace around the template you have chosen. A template that is at least 12 inches (30.5 cm) in diameter creates a pouch that works well for most purposes.

2. Cut out the circle with scissors.

3. Punch evenly spaced holes around the circumference of the circle. Put the edge of the chamois as far as it will go in your paper punch. Try to maintain this distance all around the circle.

4. Thread your cord through one hole, then weave the cord in and out of the holes around the circle. Leave a tail of cord hanging from where you started.

5. When you have woven through all the holes, match the ends of the cord and tie them with an overhand knot. Pull the cord to gather the material.

WHAT YOU NEED
(FOR COINS)

- 2-ounce (56 g) blocks of metallic-colored polymer clay in gold, bronze, and silver
- table knife
- resealable sandwich bags
- rolling pin or straight-sided jar
- shaping and texturing tools: fork, fancy silver spoons, Phillips head screws, embossed metal beads, bottle caps, jar lids, coins, toothpicks
- colored pencils (optional)
- photocopies of images (optional)
- cookie sheet covered with aluminium foil
- oven
- hot pads

INSTRUCTIONS
(FOR COINS)

1. For each color that you are using, use half a block of polymer clay. Cut the clay with the table knife. Store the other half in a resealable sandwich bag to use another time.

2. Knead the clay in your hands. Roll it into a ball and stretch it out. Repeat this action until the clay is warm and soft.

3. Roll the clay into a ball and then flatten it with the palm of your hand. Use the rolling pin or straight-sided jar to flatten the ball into a thin sheet about $1/4$ inch (6 mm) thick.

4. For round coins, use a bottle cap to cut circles from the sheet. For larger round coins, use a small jar lid. For more unusual shapes, see what kind of cookie cutters you have around the house, or use the table knife to cut triangles, squares, etc.

Decorating Ideas

5. There are many ways you can decorate the coins:

- The tines of a fork and the fancy handles of old silver spoons can create interesting looking indentations around the edge of the coin.

- Phillips head screws and embossed metal beads make attractive paterns, too.

CONTINUED ON PAGE 34

33

CONTINUED FROM PAGE 33

• Use the end of a toothpick to carve patterns on the coin.

• You can also roll small balls or coils of a second color of clay and add them to the surface of the coins.

• After the coins are baked, you can use colored pencils to decorate them, too.

• If you're feeling full of energy, you can make photocopies of signs or symbols you would like on your coins (for instance, the alchemical symbols for gold, silver, and copper). Cut out the photocopied designs to fit the face of your coin, and follow steps 4 and 6 described in the Magic Amulet on pages 22 and 23.

6. Carefully place the coins on the cookie sheet. Bake your coins for 10 minutes according to the manufacturer's instructions on the package of polymer clay. Use the hot pads to remove the cookie sheet from the oven. When the coins have cooled, carry them in the reticule (page 33).

The Giant Rat of Sumatra, Poison Toads, and Other Thoroughly Unsuitable

WIZARD'S FAMILIARS

A rat the size of a large cat? A toad as heavy as a brick? Would you choose either to be your familiar, your animal companion and helpmate? Some wizards prefer the common garden toad or handy pocket-sized rat. But the choice is yours. And if big is what you're after, try the white Sprague-Dawley or dark-on-white Wistar rats: they grow to about 8 inches (20.3 cm). That's a lot of rat! If your taste is more exotic, consider *Rhizomys sumatrensis*, the great Sumatran bamboo rat. My good friend, the famous English detective Sherlock Holmes, called his horrible memory of the giant rat of Sumatra "a story for which the world is not yet prepared." Even the young Hardy Boys had a brush with it in one of their adventures. With a body some 19 inches (48.3 cm) long and a tail of equal length, this giant rat dwarfs your average black or brown rat. Imagine it loose in a dark room!

Cricetomys gambianus, the giant African pouched rat, is almost as big and is kept by many non-wizards as a gentle house pet. This rat loves to collect baubles, such as buttons and coins,

carrying them around in its cheek pouches. If you get a rat with one pink eye and one black or dark ruby eye, name him Odd Eye.

For centuries, toads and hunchbacks were thought to ward off the power of the evil eye, soaking up its venomous rays, while frogs symbolized abundance. And as everyone knows, many frogs are actually princes in disguise! Or maybe it's that you have to kiss a lot of frogs to get a prince, or so my sister sorceresses tell me.

Toads may be more your cup of tea, but even wizards should beware the poisonous giant toad (*Bufo marinus*), also known as the cane toad. This warty monster eats anything it can swallow, including small mammals. It weighs more than 2 pounds (1 kg) and measures almost 18 inches (45.7 cm) including its legs. Nastiest of all, bulging sacs behind its eyes carry a poison so toxic it seriously harms humans and kills dogs or cats who try to eat the toad. If size interests you the most, consider instead the foot-long (30 cm), nonpoisonous goliath frog of West Africa, or the tiniest frog in the world, the Psyllophryne didactyla of Brazil, measuring only a hair over $1/3$ inch (8 mm).

High-Speed Chase Broom

Don't despair! You won't ruin a perfectly good broom by converting it into a supersonic broom for high-altitude chases. After you've angled the broomcorn, the shape is also perfect for capturing dust bunnies behind your desk and underneath the couch.

But just to be on the safe side, be sure to ask an adult wizard in the house if it's okay to transform their favorite broom from sweeper to swooper.

WHAT YOU NEED

- broom with wooden handle
- black marker
- newspaper or plastic sheeting to cover work surface
- large scissors
- acrylic paints in gold, silver, copper, or the colors of your choice
- paintbrush
- reflective tape
- plastic milk jug (emptied & cleaned)
- photocopy of wing stabilizer on page 36
- masking tape
- craft knife
- hammer
- small tacks
- hot glue gun and glue sticks
- bicycle reflectors

INSTRUCTIONS

1. Lay the broom on the floor. Use the marker to draw an angled line from one side of the top of the broomcorn at the stitching line to the opposite corner at the bottom of the broomcorn (figure 1 on page 36).

2. Cut the broomcorn on the marked line. Cut one layer at a time until the broomcorn is angled as pictured. You

can trim the edge flush with the scissors when you have cut through all the layers (figure 2).

3. Cover a flat work surface with newspaper or plastic sheeting. Lay the broom down and paint one side of the wooden handle in the color you have chosen. Allow to dry. Turn the broom over and paint the other side of the broom handle. Allow to dry. Paint each side with a second coat if desired.

4. Use the broomcorn stitching as a guide to paint stripes or a flame design (see figure 3) on the broomcorn. This design can match the color of the handle or you can use a different color altogether. You could also paint the name of the broom on the handle (my last chase broom was called Thundercloud).

5. Secure the end of a roll of reflective tape at the bottom of the broom handle and wind the tape diagonally up the handle. Cut off the tape when you reach the top.

6. Use a copy machine to enlarge the winged stabilizer pattern to fit your broom (figure 4). Then cut it out. Tape the pattern to the milk jug, wrapping it around the corner.

FIGURE 1

Trace around the pattern with a marker. Use a craft knife to cut out the shape. Then make straight slits on the shape, as shown in figure 4.

7. Paint the winged stabilizer with acrylic paint, and allow it to dry. Then, thread the end of the broom handle through the slits you have cut. Position the winged stabilizer on the handle and secure it with one or two small tacks.

8. Glue on the small bicycle reflectors.

FIGURE 2

FIGURE 4

FIGURE 3

Sorcerer Slipovers

These fanciful slipover shoes are easy to make with felt, needle and thread, and a few measurements. Decorate them with glitter paint, glue on colorful designs, or leave them plain for workaday wizard chores.

WHAT YOU NEED

- $1/4$ yard (22.9 cm) of felt or four 9 x 12-inch (22.9 x 30.5 cm) rectangles of craft felt
- measuring tape
- pencil and paper
- piece of copier paper, 11 x 17 inches (27.9 x 43.2 cm)
- ruler
- scissors
- straight pins
- sewing needle
- sewing thread or metallic embroidery floss
- self-adhesive hook-and-loop tape
- felt scraps
- fusible webbing or fabric glue
- glitter puffy paint
- 2 plastic grocery bags

INSTRUCTIONS

1. Use a measuring tape to measure around the bottom of your shoe. Write this measurement down on a piece of paper. Label it A. As you make the measurements in steps 2 through 4, write them down on a sheet of paper.

2. With your foot flat on the floor, measure the distance from the floor over the arch of your shoe at the highest point. Label this measurement B.

3. With your foot still flat on the floor, measure the distance from the floor over the widest part of the shoe at the base of the toes. Label this measurement C.

4. Measure from the floor to the top of the back of your shoe. Label this measurement D.

5. Take measurement A, add 1 inch (2.5 cm), and divide by 2. Measure

and draw a line along the long edge of your paper. This is the bottom of the shoe.

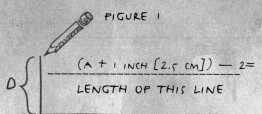

FIGURE 1

$$\frac{(A + 1 \text{ INCH } [2.5 \text{ CM}]) - 2}{\text{LENGTH OF THIS LINE}} =$$

D {

6. Mark a point equal to measurement D perpendicular to the line in step 5. This will become the back of your shoe (see figure 1).

7. Find the halfway point of the line in step 5. Make a perpendicular line equal to measurement B at this point.

8. Draw a line halfway between the line in step 7 and the end of the slipover. Make this line equal to measurement C.

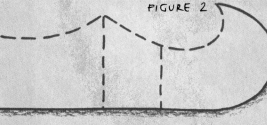

FIGURE 2

9. Connect the lines you have marked, as shown in figure 2. Draw the curved toe as shown, or create a toe shaped like a unicorn's horn (mine are shaped like the horn of a young rhinoceros). This becomes your slipover pattern.

10. Cut out the pattern. Pin the pattern to a piece of felt. Carefully cut out the felt along the edge of the pattern. Repeat until you have four pieces cut out.

11. Match the edges of two pieces and pin them together. Use a whipstitch to sew the two pieces together from point X to Y (see figure 3).

12. Sew the other shoe.

13. Try on the slipover over your shoe. Adjust to fit, and use a pencil to mark where the backs overlap.

14. Measure and cut two lengths of hook-and-loop tape the same length as measurement D.

15. Put the hook side of the hook-and-loop tape on the outside back of the slipover at the mark you made in step 13. Put the loop side of the tape on the inside edge of the opposite side.

16. Repeat steps 14 and 15 for the other shoe.

17. Decorate the sides of the shoes as desired. You can copy and transfer some of the designs in this book onto felt scraps; then cut them out, and use iron-on fusible webbing or fabric glue to attach them to the shoes. You can also paint some of these designs on the shoes with glitter puffy paint.

18. Stuff the curled point of each shoe with a wadded-up plastic grocery bag. This will help them keep their shape.

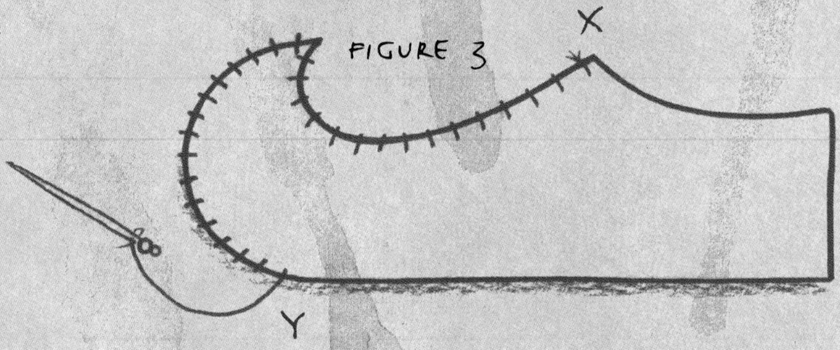

FIGURE 3

X

Y

Solomon's Magic Ring

*Gleaming glass jewel
shiny golden string.
Justice and kindness
should rule the hand
of he who wears this ring.*

In A.D. 100 to 400 there lived an extraordinary wizard named King Solomon. There are many stories about his wisdom and power. He possessed a magic ring with which he commanded spirits, called the *djinn*, to do his bidding. The ring I describe here is a beauty but it has fairly low wattage, which makes it suitable for novice wizards and sorceresses. But who can tell? Try commanding your younger brother to do your Saturday chores. If that works, the ring may be more powerful than I remember.

WHAT YOU NEED

- 18-gauge or finer brass or copper wire*
- ruler
- wire cutters*
- dowel or stick 6 inches (15 cm) long and about the width of the finger you want to wear the ring on
- flat-nose pliers*
- large glass marble or flat marble jewel
- transparent or masking tape

*sold in craft stores

INSTRUCTIONS

1. To make your ring, you will size and shape the wire by wrapping it around a mandrel—a wooden dowel or stick that's as wide as the finger you'll wear the ring on.

2. Measure and cut off 24 inches (61 cm) of wire. Tightly and closely coil the wire six times around the mandrel (figure 1 on page 40). Slide the wire off the mandrel.

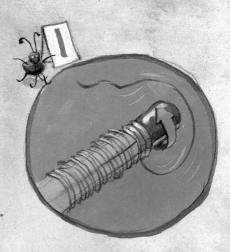

Use the flat-nose pliers to pull the wire tightly (figure 2). Continue wrapping the wire around the ring until you reach the point where you began.

4. Place your marble or glass jewel on the ring. Wrap the long end of the wire over the marble and down.

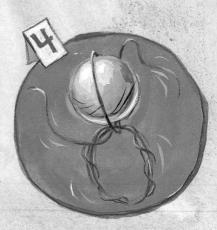

3. Starting at the point where the coil begins, wrap the long end of the wire around the coils holding them together (figure 2).

6. Wind the wire down through the ring again. Then, tightly wrap the wire around and around the base of the marble to secure it in place (figure 5). Cut off any excess wire.

Hold the wire to the marble temporarily with a 1-inch (2.5 cm) piece of tape (figure 3).

5. Bring the wire through the ring, then bring it up again to cross the marble. You may continue crossing the wire over the marble as many times as you wish (figure 4).

Wizard's Trunk

A simple cardboard storage box purchased from a discount or hardware store is easily transformed into a trunk for storing your wizard regalia when you're not using it. You can buy cardboard storage boxes in a variety of colors, wood grains, and patterns. The choice is yours.

WHAT YOU NEED

- corrugated cardboard storage box with removable lid
- heavy aluminum foil oven liner
- scissors
- pencil
- ruler
- white craft glue
- scrap paper
- acrylic paints
- paintbrushes
- ballpoint pen
- marking pens

HERE ARE A FEW IDEAS FOR PERSONALIZING YOUR TRUNK.

1. Use scissors to cut eight rectangles measuring 2 x 6 inches (5 x 15 cm) from an aluminum foil oven liner. Round each end of a foil rectangle. Use the ballpoint pen to create several small circles at the ends of each rectangle; these become the "nail heads." Emboss the circles following the general directions for embossing on page 130. Glue two embossed rectangles around each corner of the trunk.

2. Create a personalized label for the trunk by cutting a shape of your choice from the oven liner. Copy your name onto a scrap of paper using the runic alphabet on page 94. Hold the piece of paper against a window, with the writing side pressed against the glass. Then trace the reversed letters with a pencil. Use this pattern to emboss your name on the label. Glue the label on to the trunk.

3. If you are feeling particularly industrious, try making a mock lock from the scraps of the foil liner.

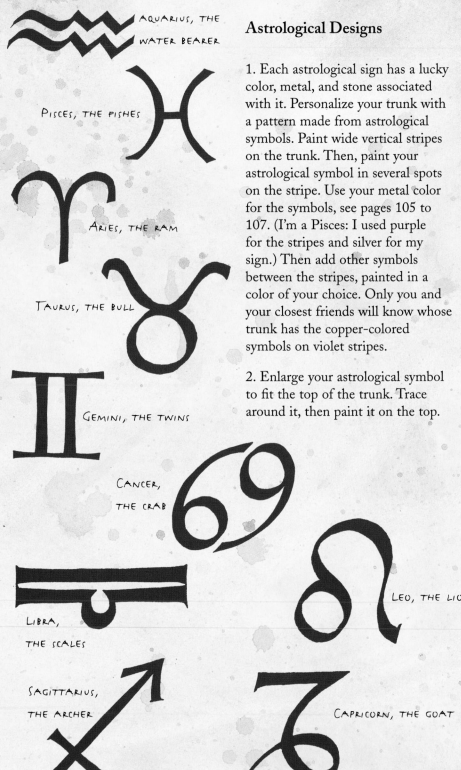

AQUARIUS, THE WATER BEARER

PISCES, THE FISHES

ARIES, THE RAM

TAURUS, THE BULL

GEMINI, THE TWINS

CANCER, THE CRAB

LIBRA, THE SCALES

LEO, THE LION

VIRGO, THE VIRGIN

SCORPIO, THE SCORPION

SAGITTARIUS, THE ARCHER

CAPRICORN, THE GOAT

Astrological Designs

1. Each astrological sign has a lucky color, metal, and stone associated with it. Personalize your trunk with a pattern made from astrological symbols. Paint wide vertical stripes on the trunk. Then, paint your astrological symbol in several spots on the stripe. Use your metal color for the symbols, see pages 105 to 107. (I'm a Pisces: I used purple for the stripes and silver for my sign.) Then add other symbols between the stripes, painted in a color of your choice. Only you and your closest friends will know whose trunk has the copper-colored symbols on violet stripes.

2. Enlarge your astrological symbol to fit the top of the trunk. Trace around it, then paint it on the top.

POLTERGEISTS & THEIR MISCHIEF

WOOWOWOWOOOOOOWOWOOWOWO · GET OUT OF THIS HOUSE!

Windows, doors, and drawers open and shut by themselves. Lights turn on and off, and bad smells or loud noises erupt for no reason. Stones, dirt, or small objects rain down on you out of the blue, or your granny's wig flies from her head and across the room. Your piano or refrigerator suddenly decides to take a walk across the floor, and the TV turns itself on. Your computer starts displaying strange messages, and you have no idea how they got there.

What on earth is happening? You've probably got a poltergeist in the house, and you have my sympathy.

Frequently mischievous and sometimes mean, poltergeists have been causing a ruckus since ancient times. Poltergeists are different from ghosts. Their name comes from the German *poltern* (to knock) and *geist* (spirit). They usually show up at night, and can come and go in a matter of minutes, or stay around for months or years. They seem to be particularly attracted to homes where teenage girls live. Some researchers think the physical events might actually be caused by the mental energies of a person living in the house.

There are hundreds of poltergeist stories from all around the world.

One of the earliest reports dates from A.D. 355 and describes sleeping people being thrown out of their beds in Bingen-am-Rhein, Germany.

In 1661, in the famous case of the Drummer of Tedworth, an English justice of the peace ordered a drummer to stop playing his drum because the noise annoyed village residents. After the drum was taken to a house in the nearby village of Tedworth for safekeeping, drumming, storms, panting, foul odors, scratchings, and other disturbances erupted inside the house, lasting for two years.

A 1715 letter from the mother of John Wesley, founder of the Methodist church, describes groans and other signs from a poltergeist at their home, the Rectory at Epworth, England. Old Jeffrey, as the family nicknamed the presence, finally went away after two months.

In 1817, a poltergeist started bothering the Bell family of Robertson County, Tennessee. It used to throw sticks and stones at the children on their way to school; in a strange kind of game, the children and the poltergeist threw the missiles back and forth at each other!

A 1973 report from Paraguay describes how a poltergeist removed a baby carriage (with the baby sleeping inside) from a house and deposited it under a tree outside, baby still safely sleeping!

In 1977 at an ordinary house in north London, the Enfield poltergeist tormented the Hodgson family, moving around furniture, throwing hairbrushes, and writing messages on walls. It finally left a year and a half later.

In 1981, slamming doors, weird noises, and coins flying across rooms finally convinced a young couple to move out of their house in Kent, England.

So is a poltergeist truly an unseen visitor, or the projected mental energies of a teenager? Scientists don't know, and they continue to study the matter. My advice? If a poltergeist comes to visit your house, remember that it won't stay forever, and it can be friendly. But if a hairbrush comes sailing at you, don't forget to duck!

Chapter 2

THE DECORATIVE ARTS

Our home is our castle, and you'll want to make sure your room looks like a wizard lives there. I found the crystal ball on page 53 to be most useful, and, when you're not gazing into it to see what's to come, it makes a handy bedside light. I picked up my first flying carpet when I was in Arabia, and Ali Baba the rug merchant kindly told me how to make another one. I pass his instructions on to you. Of course we all need a magic looking glass for our chamber, and if you really want to impress your wizard friends, you can make a photograph that shows the past, present, and future, depending on how you look at it. You'll find my secrets for making these things and more in this chapter.

WITH MY NEW SKILLS, I QUICKLY LEARNED

TO ENTERTAIN MYSELF AND MY FRIENDS.

Magic Carpet

If you can't travel to Istanbul to buy a magic carpet from a Sufi master, you can make your own after a quick trip to your local discount and craft stores. Just imagine how much fun it would be to fly over the minarets (or your local wizard supply store) if this carpet was truly magical. Or perhaps you won't have to imagine...

WHAT YOU NEED

- small, washable throw rug*
- photocopy of minaret template, page 142
- scissors
- pencil
- sheets of newspaper
- ruler
- fabric paints in colors of your choice
- paintbrushes, 1 inch (2.5 cm) wide
- 2 yards (1.8 m) upholstery or drapery fringe
- fabric glue
- needle and thread (optional)

*Notes about rugs: Look for flat pile or woven rugs made for the kitchen and bath. If your rug has a pattern, turn it over and decorate the back side. You can also use carpet remnants with low pile. Some craft stores sell pre-hemmed canvas floorcloths which you can also use; you'll just have to paint a background color on the canvas.

INSTRUCTIONS

1. If your rug is washable, wash it before you begin painting and adding the fringe.

2. Enlarge the minaret design (page 142) on a photocopy machine so that you can fit two or more on your rug.

3. Cut out the design. Place it on the rug, and trace around it with a pencil. Repeat this until you like the arrangement of minarets on your rug.

4. Cover your work surface with newspaper.

5. Paint the minarets with your choice of color.

6. Paint curlicues freehand around the minarets; paint them small or large, the choice is up to you.

7. Measure and cut lengths of fringe the width of your rug. Attach a length of fringe with fabric glue, weight the fringe with heavy books, and allow it to dry. Repeat for the opposite side. If you want, you can sew the fringe to the rug.

Mirror of Fantasy

Hephaestus (the famous ancient Greek metalworker) created my original magic mirror framed in silver and studded with precious jewels. You can create a replica that mimics metalwork without having to use an anvil or forge.

WHAT YOU NEED

- small mirror (square or rectangular)*
- photocopy of pattern on page 48
- corrugated cardboard (recycle a box)
- pencil
- scissors or craft knife
- ruler
- aluminum foil
- hot glue gun and glue sticks
- black, brown, or dark blue acrylic paint
- paintbrush
- paper towels or rag
- felt or cardboard to cover the mirror back
- self-adhesive picture hanger
- glass or plastic jewels

*Buy inexpensive mirrors in drugstores or hardware stores. Have an adult help you remove any existing frame.

INSTRUCTIONS

1. Copy and enlarge the patterns on page 48 to fit the corner of your mirror. Cut out the pattern copies.

2. Lay the pattern on a sheet of cardboard. Trace around the pattern with a pencil. Repeat until you have four separate shapes. Use scissors or a craft knife to cut out all four shapes.

3. Position the four shapes on the corners of the mirror. Use a ruler to measure the length and width of the area your mirror and shapes cover.

4. Measure and mark a shape to the measurements in step 3. Cut this shape out with scissors or a craft knife.

5. Roll out a sheet of aluminum foil long enough to wrap completely around both sides of the flat rectangle of cardboard. Smooth the foil around the cardboard.

6. Use hot glue to attach the four template shapes to the corners of the foil-covered cardboard. After you have glued the shapes, set the mirror in place to check the position of the shapes. Remove the mirror.

7. Roll out a length of aluminum foil slightly longer than the flat piece of cardboard. Gently crumple the foil in your hands and then carefully flatten it out on a flat surface.

8. Lay the slightly crumpled foil on the cardboard. Use your fingers to make the foil conform to the shapes. Work slowly: if you work too fast or press too hard, you will tear the foil. Fold the excess foil to the back of the frame.

9. Pour a little acrylic paint onto a scrap of cardboard. Brush paint on a small section of the frame, then wipe off the excess with a paper towel or rag to antique the surface. Antique the surface of the entire frame until you like the way that it looks. Allow it to dry.

10. Hot glue the mirror to the frame.

11. Measure and cut a piece of felt or cardboard large enough to cover the back of the frame. Hot glue this to the back of the frame. Attach the self-adhesive picture hanger to the back of the frame.

12. Hot glue the jewels to the front of the frame as desired.

PHOTOCOPY THESE PATTERNS TO CREATE DECORATIVE CORNERS FOR YOUR MIRROR.

Floating Magic Candle

Every self-respecting wizard's chamber needs to have a floating candle or two! This candle is particularly magical because it will burn all the way to the end while still floating in the water! BEFORE YOU START, ASK THE ADULT WIZARD OF YOUR HOUSE IF YOU CAN MAKE IT. When you burn the candle, make sure it's in a safe place and never leave the flame unattended.

WHAT YOU NEED

• candle, 5 inches (13 cm) long,
3/4 inch (1.9 cm) wide*
• wood screw, 1 inch (2.5 cm) long
• glass canning jar,
1-quart (.95 L) size
• water
• food coloring
(optional)
• matches

INSTRUCTIONS

1. Screw the wood screw slightly into the flat end of the candle, making sure the screw is straight and not bending toward one side or the other.

2. Fill the jar with water to 1 inch (2.5 cm) below the brim. If you want, you can add a few drops of food coloring to turn the water your favorite color.

3. Holding the candle by the wick, slowly lower it into the water, screw end first. The candle should float freely without touching the bottom of the jar, its wick end above the surface of the water. Loosen your grip on the wick slightly to check that the top won't tip over into the water. If the candle starts to tip over, try a heavier screw in the bottom.

4. Light the candle with a match.

*These are often sold as emergency candles, and they come in packs of four.

Crossbones Board

Every wizard needs a handy place to jot down notes, reminders, or messages. Otherwise, he could forget to pick up an ounce of bat hairs the next time he's in the village. The crossbones that decorate the frame of this chalkboard will make the "DO NOT ENTER" message for your little brother more threatening.

WHAT YOU NEED

- framed slate board*
- 2-ounce (56 g) block of white or ivory-colored polymer clay
- flat work surface
- cookie sheet covered with aluminum foil
- oven
- hot pads
- white craft glue

*Framed slate boards are sold in most craft stores.

INSTRUCTIONS

1. Knead the block of clay in your hands. Roll it into a ball and stretch it out. Repeat this action until the clay is warm and soft.

2. Pull a small ball of clay from the block of clay. Roll it between the palms of your hands until you have a coil about the size of your little finger. Add more clay to the coil if needed. Make a second coil the same size as the first.

3. Put the coils on a flat surface. Cross them to make X-shapes. Lightly flatten them on the flat surface. You want the tops of the coils rounded slightly. Smooth together the edges where the coils cross with your fingers.

4. Pinch off very small bits of clay and roll eight small balls. Put two on the end of each coil to create a bonelike shape. Smooth the edges where they meet the coil so that they look like they are a part of the coil.

5. Make three more of these cross-bone shapes.

6. Carefully place the crossbones on the cookie sheet. Bake the bones for about 15 minutes according to the manufacturer's instructions on the package of polymer clay. Use hot pads to remove the cookie sheet from the oven. Let the bones cool completely.

7. Use white glue to attach the crossbones to each corner of the frame.

Draco & Other Serpents of the Skies

Draco the Dragon was the mightiest constellation in the night sky 4,000 years ago.

A group of stars shaped like a long serpent with a triangular head, Draco was the pole star of ancient times, the center point of the evening sky. The Egyptians called it Thuban; the Persians called it Ashdeha, a man-eating serpent; and the Hindus called it Shi-shu-mara, a giant alligator. But in ancient times, to the people who watched the sky night after night as the seasons changed, the planets and stars seemed to revolve around Draco. In Egypt 3,000 years ago, the great pyramid of Khufu at Gizeh was built so that Draco could always be seen from the bottom of the air shafts that traveled deep into the mysterious heart of the pyramid. The stars have shifted, and today the pole star is Polaris. But mighty Draco still glitters.

The Greeks said that Draco was fixed in the sky when the goddess Athena fought evil giants in a 10-year battle. A giant threw a dragon at Athena, and she tossed it into the North sky, where it came to rest. Even earlier Babylonian stories tell of an evil sea serpent named Tiamat, which was responsible for the dark chaos that made up the world before the earth and heavens were created. New gods arose to bring order to the world, and Tiamat battled them with the help of other horrible sea monsters, poisonous serpents, and men shaped like scorpions. Marduk, a hero who was given magical powers by the gods, fought Tiamat with the help of winds from heaven. Tiamat was torn to shreds, and Marduk the Dragon Slayer built heaven, earth, and the constellations.

Hercules is part of the legend of the serpent constellation Hydra, the Many-Headed Monster. The huge, nine-headed water snake lived in a swamp. Its blood was poisonous, and its breath could kill instantly. The hero tried to kill the monster, but every time he cut off one of its heads, another one would grow back in its place! Finally, Hercules used a flaming torch to seal the wounds as he cut off the heads,

preventing new heads from forming. Even though a giant crab came out of the swamp to help Hydra, Hercules finally won by cutting off the snake's one special head that could live forever.

Another old legend says that Hydra was formed by the god Apollo, angry that his pet raven was delayed in bringing him a cup of water. The raven had stopped to eat fruit, then brought back a water snake to its master, claiming the snake caused the delay. Apollo saw through the lie, and threw bird, cup, and snake into the skies. Crater (The Cup) and Corvus (the Raven) can be seen perched on the serpent's back in the sky.

Ophiuchus is the constellation known as the Serpent-Holder and the Serpent. Its name comes from the story of Aesculapius, who discovered the healing power of herbs when he saw a snake give a sprig of herb to another snake that seemed dead, and the dead snake recovered. Aesculapius studied herbs and used his knowledge to cure sick people. Hades, god of the underworld, complained to his brother Zeus that since the doctor was many people and bringing them from the dead, fewer were the underworld. Zeus he killed Aesculapius with a thunderbolt. But because admired the doctor's talents made him into a constellation, along with the taught him the healing herbs. Today, own symbol for is still

Bats and Stars

Twinkle twinkle soaring bat
How I wonder where you're at.
Up above you're quite a sight.
At first you caused me quite a fright!

Twinkle twinkle little star.
What'ya doing up so far?
From where I lie here in my room
could I reach you on my broom?

WHAT YOU NEED

- **photocopies of bat and star patterns (page 141)**
- **star pattern**
- **tracing paper**
- **pencil**
- **scissors**
- **poster board, black and metallic silver or gold**
- **wooden or acrylic cutting board**
- **craft knife**
- **fishing line (monofilament wire)**
- **white craft glue**
- **thumbtacks**
- **masking tape (optional)**

INSTRUCTIONS

1. Photocopy and enlarge the bat and star patterns, and then cut them out with the scissors.

2. Place the bat shape on the black poster board and trace around it. Repeat until you have traced 30 bat shapes.

3. Place the star shape on the silver or gold poster board and trace around it. Repeat until you have traced 30 or more stars.

4. Cover your work surface with a wood or acrylic cutting board. Place the poster board on that surface, and carefully cut out the bats and stars with the craft knife.

5. Cut 30 lengths of fishing line, each 12 to 15 inches (30.5 to 38 cm).

6. Glue one end of the fishing line to the middle of one of the bat shapes. Dot glue around the edge of the bat shape and lay another bat shape on top. Repeat this with the other bat shapes until you have glued 15 bat sandwiches.

7. Now glue 15 star sandwiches.

8. With help from a ladder and an adult sorceress, climb up and tack the loose end of the fishing line to the ceiling (or use masking tape). Hang the bats and stars over your bed.

Glowing Crystal Ball

Most of the materials for this project can be found at a hardware or home improvement store, or a local lamp shop. If you are not comfortable with the electrical arts, a lamp shop can put together the lamp for a reasonable cost. Or you can leave out the lamp parts and—with help from the magic available to us all—let your imagination illuminate the ball.

WHAT YOU NEED

- clear glass globe (used for lighting fixtures, see step 1 on page 54)
- glass cleaner
- paper towels
- patterns on page 142
- tracing paper
- pencil
- scissors
- clear adhesive shelf paper
- interior glass frosting spray OR glass etching gel or liquid*
- newspaper to cover work area
- lamp kit (candelabra size)
- small, low-wattage light bulb
- wooden lamp base the same size as the open end of the globe

*sold in most craft stores

INSTRUCTIONS

1. Clean the globe with glass cleaner and set it aside.

2. Trace the patterns on page 142, or use other designs you like, such as crescent moons or dragons. Cut out your designs, as shown in figure 2.

3. Transfer these cutout designs to the clear adhesive shelf paper by tracing around them. Then cut out these shapes. See figure 3.

5. Whenever you use etching gel or frosting spray, you should work in a room that gets plenty of fresh air. Better yet, move this part of the project outdoors! In either case, be sure to cover your work surface with newspaper.

Contact Paper

covered with the adhesive shapes will still be clear glass, but all the rest of the glass will be etched or frosted.

4. Peel the backing from the clear adhesive shelf paper, and put the sticky cutout design on the glass-globe. If you don't like the position, you can carefully peel it up and move it. Repeat this with all the shapes (figure 4).

Carefully read the instructions that come with the etching gel or frosting spray you bought. Apply the product to the globe as described on the package. See figure 5.

6. After the globe is frosted or etched, carefully remove the clear adhesive designs. The areas of the globe that were

7. Have a trained professional wire the base for you with a small, candelabra fixture: This is not something a young wizard should play around with! Screw a small light bulb in the fixture and then set the globe on the wired base.

The HAND OF GLORY,

or Some People Are Unbelievably Stupid

I never, ever approved of this practice, but back in the dark time of the Middle Ages, a few people created candleholders from hands cut from hanged men. The purpose was evil magic, and no self-respecting good wizard would have anything to do with it.

After it was rendered of its fat, then spiced, pickled, and dried, the so-called Hand of Glory resembled a mummy's hand. The fat from the hand was used to make a candle (forget about getting a recipe from me for this, I told you I don't approve). With the lighted candle fixed in its grip, the Hand's light was believed to paralyze anyone who saw it.

The Hand could also be used to cast a spell over a sleeping person, making him sleep for a whole day without waking. Either way, it was very handy for thieves and cowards who didn't want to get caught at whatever they were doing.

Amazing how these beliefs hang on.

In 1831, in County Neath, Ireland, some thieves actually woke up an outraged squire and his entire family, who caught the burglars red-handed, so to speak, trying to rob the house by the light of a Hand of Glory. They ran away, leaving the Hand behind, and the whole lot of them probably ended up in jail. Just remember that sometimes it doesn't take magic to correct wrongdoing, only a well-timed word to the police. But don't tell anybody I said that, and no, I don't remember if I happened to be in that part of Ireland that particular night.

Past, Present, and Future Picture Show

Amaze your friends with this three-way picture. The past, present, and future can be shown with a baby picture, a current snapshot, and a photo of yourself in wizard regalia. Any three images cut to the same size can be used. If you like a challenge, you can choose pictures that show movement or time passing.

WHAT YOU NEED

- 3 snapshots of the same size that you don't mind cutting up*
- 18 x 25-inch (45.7 x 63.5 cm) sheet of construction paper
- ruler
- pencil

- scissors
- glue stick
- wax paper
- heavy books
- poster board

*If you need to, you can enlarge your snapshots on a color photocopier. It costs only a few wizard coins to use these copiers.

INSTRUCTIONS

1. Lay the three snapshots on top of the sheet of construction paper and trace around them (figure 1). If your pictures are big, you may need to glue on additional paper to make the piece long enough. Put the photos aside.

2. Mark the length of paper in ¹/₂-inch (1.3 cm) increments along the top and bottom edges. Use the straight edge of the ruler and a pencil to connect the marks (figure 2).

3. Fold up the strip of paper along the marked lines like a fan, with every third strip remaining

flat while the others are
pushed together
(figure 3).

4. Number the 1/2-inch (1.3 cm) increments 1, 2, and 3. Repeat across the entire strip (figure 4).

5. Measure and mark 1/2-inch increments on the top and

bottom edges of each picture. Connect the marks, as before.

6. Determine which is the "past" picture. Begin to cut 1/2-inch strips from that picture. Use the glue stick generously to glue a picture strip onto the spaces numbered with 1.

You'll be tempted to go ahead and cut all of the strips, but don't; it's easy to mix up the strips (figure 5).

7. Repeat step 6 with the "present" picture, and glue it to the strips marked 3. Repeat step 6 with the "future" picture, and glue it to the strips marked 2.

8. When all the strips are glued, cover the papers with wax paper, and weight them with heavy books. Allow the strips to dry for one hour.

9. Measure and mark a piece of poster board to the width of one of your pictures.

Refold the strip with the glued-on pictures as you did in step 3.

10. Spread a coat of glue on the poster board and place the folded picture on top. Squeeze together strips 1 and 2. Glue strip 3 flat on the poster board. Repeat along the length of the picture. Trim any excess poster board at the end.

Magic Lantern

Time to shine some light
as signs of day take flight.
Stars are filling up the sky.
On this lamp I can rely.
New moon, full moon
in my nightime room.

WHAT YOU NEED

- lamp with white paper or fabric shade
- acrylic paint in color of your choice
- paintbrush
- patterns on pages 141 to 142
- pencil
- tracing paper
- scissors
- adhesive shelf paper
- tape

INSTRUCTIONS

1. Paint the inside of the lamp shade and let dry.

2. Trace the patterns that you want to use. Or you can use other designs you like. Cut them out.

3. Tape the shapes onto the adhesive shelf paper, trace around them, and cut them out of the adhesive shelf paper.

4. Paint the non-sticky side of the adhesive shelf paper the same color as the inside of the lamp shade. Let dry.

5. Peel off the backing layer of the adhesive shelf paper, and stick the patterns in place inside the shade. During the day, when the light is switched off, you will not see the patterns. But come nightime when you turn on the light, the patterns will suddenly, magically appear.

WHO'S THERE?!!!

Screaming Skulls and the Ghosts of Famous Headless People

Many perfectly ordinary houses are haunted, and the people who live in them report visits from the supernatural even in broad daylight. But our really well-known ghosts tend to be associated with ancient British manors, castles and abbeys. Many of them are the ghosts of men and women who lost their heads to the executioner's axe. Most unfortunate. Then there are the tales of the heads that lost their bodies, the infamous screaming skulls...

Some ancient homes possess skulls that simply refuse to leave. The skull of a Catholic priest executed for treason in 1641 resides at Wardley Hall near Manchester, England. The priest's head was displayed as a warning after his execution, then taken to the Hall where it remained on view for many years. When one owner tried to bury it, violent storms broke out. When it was thrown into a pond, it reappeared again at the Hall.

The screaming skull of Bettiscombe Manor in Dorset, England, did much the same, and more. In legend, the skull belonged to the West Indian slave of an heir of the manor. The slave's owner promised that the slave's body would be returned to Africa for burial when he died, but he broke his promise and buried it in a local churchyard instead. After mysterious groans and shrieks kept the family awake for weeks, they moved the body back to the loft of the manor. After many years, only the skull remained. Whenever it was taken from the manor, thunderstorms destroyed crops and cattle died. Buried nine feet deep in the ground, the skull worked its way to the surface the next day, waiting to be taken home. Taken to the attic, the skull "screamed like a trapped rat," according to one youth's account. Scientific examination found the skull to be prehistoric in origin, perhaps the relic of an ancient burial where the manor now stands. Slave or not, the manor owners now refuse to remove the skull from the house. Who can blame them?

For sheer quantity of ghosts of the beheaded, you can't beat the Tower of London in England, which was an infamous site of imprisonment and execution for hundreds of years. Many of the victims were like young Anne Boleyn, the second wife of King Henry VIII, who was beheaded for treason. Anne's pale figure wanders the Tower grounds, with and without her head, and guards spotted her in the Tower chapel where she is buried. Margaret, Countess of Salisbury, was beheaded at the Tower in 1541. Her shrieking ghost still runs around Tower Green, as the living Margaret did before they forced her head to the block.

Celestial Sheets

There's no reason that a wizard or sorceress can't have a well-decorated bedroom. Even if you haven't yet learned to conjure up a bed of roses to sleep on, at least you can dream up a set of celestial sheets and pillowcases and then go make them. Or if you're drawn to creatures that go flap flap in the night, you can have a bevy of bats on your bed linens. If you'd like to have wizardly wall hangings in your chamber, these will also do nicely.

WHAT YOU NEED

- sheets and pillowcases in white or solid color
- rubber stamps with large, bold designs*
- bat, star, and moon templates
- tracing paper
- carbon paper
- pencil
- rubber stamping material**
- 2-3 plastic foam meat trays
- scissors
- foam brushes with 1-inch (2.5 cm) tips
- acrylic fabric paints
- newspapers
- iron (optional)

*available in a variety of shapes, patterns, and sizes at craft stores

**thin sheets of rubber with peel-off backing; available at craft stores

INSTRUCTIONS

1. You can buy rubber stamps in craft stores, but it's fun and easy to make your own. Trace one or all of the patterns. Transfer the designs onto carbon paper. Place the carbon paper on top of the rubber stamping material, and pencil over the design again, so that the image appears on the rubber stamping material. Peel off the backing and stick the stamps onto the plastic foam meat tray. Cut out the shapes. Presto! You've just made your own stamps!

2. Decide how you want your sheets to look. Do you want just the edges of the pillowcase stamped? Does the idea of a simple band of stars (or bats) on the top edge of the sheets appeal to you more than, say, a complete galaxy over the entire sheet? Once you've decided on the pattern and color of your sheets, get them ready to work on.

3. Start with clean sheets. This is important if you have purchased new sheets—the paint won't stick well unless you wash the "sizing" out of the sheets.

4. Cover a flat work surface (the kitchen table works well) with several layers of newspaper.

5. Pour a small amount of paint into a foam tray and use a foam brush to spread paint on your stamp. Practice your stamping on a sheet of newspa-

per. When you know how much paint to brush on the stamp and how hard to press to get the image you wish, you're ready to decorate your sheets.

6. Start with a pillowcase. Place a few sheets of folded newspaper inside the pillowcase to prevent the paint from bleeding through. Smooth the fabric with your hands. Stamp your image on the pillowcase. Allow it to dry. Stamp another pillowcase if you want to.

7. Spread the top sheet on the newspaper-covered table. Stamp the image along the top edge or however you wish. If you like, you can combine the star and circle stamps, as shown in the drawing. Let each stamp dry before stamping on top of it. Let the paint dry.

8. Follow the paint manufacturer's instructions for "setting" the paint so it won't wash out.

9. NOW, GO MAKE UP YOUR BED LIKE YOUR MOTHER ASKED!

SOMETIMES A WIZARD HAS TO BE BRAVE...

WHEN ENCOUNTERING THE UNKNOWN.

Chapter 3

THE ART OF HORTICULTURE

The mandrake is probably a wizard's most essential ingredient for magic potions, and this chapter has my no-fail recipe for making as much of the magical root as you like. I'll also tell you how to plant a good magic garden, which includes several items to help you attract fairies to your home or castle. And once the Little People show up, they can relax in their own fairy pavilion and dance in a fairy circle to the music of a fairy tambourine, all built by you from instructions in this chapter. After all, how can you have magic without fairies?

Shrunken Mandrake Heads

Along with dragon's blood (see page 112 for the recipe), the mandrake is a wizard's most important magical ingredient for spells and potions. Each shrunken mandrake head has its own personality, and it's spooky how human it looks! If you store it in an airy place, it should darken with age but not spoil. If you're worried about exposure to the mandrake's deathly shriek, you can always wear earmuffs while you work.

Along with dragon's blood (see page 112 for the recipe)

WHAT YOU NEED

- large, firm apple (Golden Delicious or Granny Smith work well)
- vegetable peeler
- paring knife
- $1/2$ cup (6 g) salt
- 2 teaspoons (30 g) alum; sold in the spice section of the supermarket
- warm water
- measuring cup
- mixing bowl, in quart or liter size
- saucer (optional)
- large paper clip or length of stiff wire
- pliers
- 2 feet (60 cm) of string

INSTRUCTIONS

1. Remove the peel with the vegetable peeler, leaving a bit of peel at the top and bottom of the apple. See figure 1.

2. Use the peeler or paring knife to carve the mandrake features (figure 2). Use the tip of the knife to outline the eyes, nose, and mouth. Carve out wedge-shaped pieces from each side of the nose, and scoop out two shallow hollows for eyes. Slice a shallow slit for the mouth. Use the tip of the knife to outline semicircle "ears" on each side of the head, and cut parts of the apple from around the ears to make them stand out in relief. As you carve, be sure to make the features well-defined to allow for shrinkage as the apple dries.

3. In the mixing bowl, dissolve the salt and alum in 6 cups of warm water. Put the carved apple in the solution, and let it soak overnight. You may need to place the saucer on the apple to keep it submerged.

4. Remove the apple from the solution.

5. Straighten out the paper clip or wire, and use the tips of the pliers to form a small loop at one end of the wire. Push the straight end of the wire through the top of the apple and down through the bottom. Bend the clip or wire at the bottom to hold it in place. See figure 3.

6. Run the string through the small loop and knot it. Hang the apple from the string in a place where it will stay dry and out of direct sunlight. It will take two or three weeks for the apple to dry, depending on the humidity. You can speed the drying process a bit by placing the apple (without the wire or string) on the center rack of a warm (200°F or 93°C) oven until dry. This can take six to eight hours or more, depending on the size and the water content of the apple. As always, if you want to use the oven, ask an adult wizard to help you.

As Hamlet said, "There are more things in heaven and earth... than are dreamt of in your philosophy." Where do you think my dear friend Billy Shakespeare got all that inside information on magic and fairies and spells for the plays he wrote, such as *The Tempest* and *A Midsummer Night's Dream*? From yours truly, thank you very much! But as I was about to say, training to become a wizard means developing your ability to truly see all the things that make the world around us so special. Children and artists are naturally good at this. They understand the value of looking at a flower for half an hour, for example.

There are so many green, growing things in the world, that even I don't know all their names and uses. But you should know about some plants, flowers, and trees that pop up frequently in wizard work. Some have magical reputations, and some are interesting because they're so bizarre. And some are legendary plants known by word of mouth; but remember, we wizards are sworn to keep their location secret.

Probably the most famous magical plant is the poisonous mandrake root, known as *Mandragora officinarum* or *Atropa mandragora*. Used as an anesthetic and in ancient love potions, the mandrake was also thought to have magic powers because its forked root resembles a human body. In Germany in the 1500s, forest magicians actually dressed their mandrakes like little people, bathed them in milk, and "fed" them.

In the ancient Middle East, people believed the root drove away evil spirits. Some early craftsmen blew glass containers around the root to capture its power, like a genie in a bottle! A mandrake root could answer any question you asked it, and if you put gold coins beside the root overnight, the gold doubled by morning. On the dark side, it's said that the powerful and murderous Borgia family in Venice, Italy, used the mandrake to slowly poison its enemies.

Anyone trying to harvest a mandrake would be killed by the horrible shriek of the plant as it was pulled from the earth, so people had to be careful to cover their ears, or devise other ways to harvest the plant without hearing its cry.

Believers have always thought the blood of a dragon was the most potent ingredient you could put in a magical mixture (my personal recipe for dragon's blood is on page 112). Several hundred years ago, the "blood" came from the legendary dragon's blood tree (*Dracena draco*). The tree grows in Spain and on the nearby island of Tenerife, and other varieties are found in East Africa and South Arabia. It has a huge, hollow trunk, with swordlike leaves and branches like fleshy fingers pointing straight up. When

the trunk is gashed or wounded, a dark red resin oozes out. Craftsmen molded the hardened resin into "dragon's eggs," or carved little dragons from it. The substance was so treasured, there were many fakes on the market! Today, you can find blood grass (*Poaceae gramineae*), bloodleaf (*Amaranthaceae iresine*), bloodroot (*Sanguinaria canadensis*), and the "bloody butcher" prairie trillium flower in our forests and gardens.

Shakespeare also wrote, "A rose by any other name would smell as sweet," but would you believe there's a flower that smells like dead meat? It's called the Carrion Flower (*Asclepiadaceae stapelia*). It's a fleshy plant with five-pointed, star-shaped flowers spotted with dark purple and brown. You can grow it in pots in the full sun, but I wouldn't sit too close!

A rare and famously creepy flower is the Corpse Flower or Devil's Tongue (*Amorphophallus titanum*), the largest known flower in the world, and probably the worst-smelling. Found in the Sumatran rain forest, the flower blooms only once every 12 to 37 years. A single flower (really a collection of thousands of tiny flowers) grows more than 6 feet (1.8 m) tall and 12 feet (3.7m) around. When it does bloom, a thick, fleshy spike shoots up from the center, and the horrible smell is like a combination of rotten fish and burning sugar. I couldn't stand the foul odor for more than a few minutes, myself. After only one or two days, the flower collapses and dies, possibly never to bloom again.

Through the ages, voyagers have reported seeing fantastic trees. *Antiaris toxicaria*, The Tree of Poisons, grows on islands near China, and is reputed to emit vapors that kill plants and animals for miles around. Anyone unlucky enough to fall asleep in its shade never wakes up.

Herbalists wrote about the Barnacle Tree on the Isle of Man in Britain that opens up to release live geese!

Many travelers claimed they saw a giant tree at the site of Sodom and Gomorrah, the cities written about in the Bible. The residents were destroyed by God for their sinful ways. The huge tree bore giant "apples of Sodom" which would turn to smoke and ashes in the hands of anyone who tried to pick them, a reminder of God's lasting judgment.

Making a Terrarium with Plants that Eat Things

Did you know that some plants eat live insects and even raw meat? They're called carnivorous plants, and you can buy them in the bog garden section of your local plant store. It's easy to make an indoor terrarium where you can grow these plants, watch their remarkable activities, and feed them like pets.

Carnivorous plants can't absorb nutrients from the air and soil the way regular plants do, so they're designed to trap and eat insects and other creatures. The scientific name for the Venus flytrap is *Dionaea* and it's named after the goddess of love.

It has hinged jaws that snap shut on anything that crawls inside—including your finger—and it can eat up to three flies at a time. The sundew *(Drosera)* has dozens of slim, sticky tentacles that move to grab and glue an insect seconds after it touches one tentacle. Pitcher plants *(Sarracenia)* live in swamps. They're shaped like beautiful green and purple vases. But once a bug goes inside the lovely, curved lips, it never comes out! Trapped by hairs that point down to the bottom, the victim slips deeper and deeper, finally landing in a pool of fluid at the bottom where it's slowly digested. Nasty. Or cool, depending on your point of view.

WHAT YOU NEED

- 5-gallon (19 L) glass or clear plastic container
- small gravel
- bucket
- distilled water or rainwater collected in a bucket
- peat moss
- sand
- kitchen spoon
- Venus flytrap (*Dionaea*)
- sundew (*Drosera*)
- pitcher plant (*Sarracenia*)
- cup or watering can
- wood block or other weight
- electric light with 20-watt fluorescent bulb (optional)

and position the plants in the holes, one plant in each hole. Gently fill in the holes around the plants with dirt, covering their root systems.

5. Use the cup or watering can to gently sprinkle 1 or 2 cups (240 or 480 mL) of distilled water or rainwater inside the terrarium (figure 3). Don't use tap water or

rainwater that ran off a roof because they contain minerals harmful to the plants. Carnivorous plants like air with a high humidity level, so always keep the soil moist but not soupy. Don't close up the jar with a cap or top; leave it open to prevent fungus. Keep an eye on the plants, and if they appear to lose some of their stickiness, add more water.

6. Keep your terrarium on a windowsill (facing south is best) where it will get bright light. Use the wooden block or weight to keep it from moving. If you use an electric

light, position it at one end of the terrarium, keeping it turned on until you go to bed at night.

INSTRUCTIONS

1. Make sure your container is clean and dry, and lay it on its side. Spread a ½-inch (1.3 cm) layer of gravel on the bottom.

2. Holding a clump of the peat moss in your hand, submerge it in the bucketful of distilled water or rainwater, and squeeze all the air out of it (figure 1). This helps the peat absorb and retain water.

3. Mix together the wet peat and sand in a 2 to 1 ratio, that is, 2 cups of peat to 1 cup of sand. Spread a 2 to 3-inch (5 to 7.6 cm) layer of mix over the gravel. In the wild, carnivorous plants live in bogs in extremely poor soil, so don't add fertilizer or you'll kill the plants.

4. Use the spoon to carefully dig holes in the layer of peat and sand (figure 2),

7. Now comes the fun part! You can actually feed your Venus flytrap with small bits of raw steak by putting a piece on the end of a toothpick and gently touching it inside the plant's jaws. Or, you can catch live flies and other insects. (Try making a "bait" by putting a sugar cube inside a jar.) Release the captives inside your terrarium, and watch nature take its course.

8. Some carnivorous plants go dormant each year. Their aboveground parts die back, and it looks like the whole plant is dead. Just cut back on the watering and be patient—they'll grow back. If your plants flower, add a little mild organic fertilizer, such as fish emulsion, bone meal, or blood meal.

69

A LONG HAIRY LEG GENTLY TOUCHED ME...OR,

My Uncomfortable Encounter with the World's Biggest SPIDERS

Great wizards are great naturalists. We always befriend our animal and insect neighbors, or at least treat them with the respect you'd give an equal. After all, you never know when you'll need their help! But I have to admit even I find some species stomach-churning, as I discovered when I went to Brazil to consult with some local sorcerers.

Imagine a spider with fur, 1/2-inch (1.3 cm) fangs, a body 3 inches (7.6 cm) long, and a leg span of almost 13 inches (33 cm). This spider is aggressive and powerful enough to eat frogs, toads, lizards, mice—even the lethal Fer-de-Lance snake. It lives deep in the perpetual night of the Brazilian rain forest where you can hear it whistling and clicking. Burrowing deep in the forest floor, this arachnid doesn't like to be disturbed. If you bother it, it bites. If it can't reach you, watch out for the eight legs throwing clouds of stinging hairs.

NASTY!

Its name is the Goliath birdeater tarantula *(Theraphosa blondi)*. Worshipped by the natives of the jungle, Goliath is hard to forget, if you've ever met it. Why? Because you know Goliath is not a nightmare— it's real. And there are countless more like Goliath, waiting quietly in the forest...

We used to call tarantulas wolf spiders. They live in deserts as well as jungles. A few South American varieties build huge webs and eat live birds! Some are long-lived; one tarantula lived 30 years. It's claimed you can train tarantulas to be pets. I never have, would you?

As you walk through a field outdoors, remember it probably holds 2.5 million spiders per acre. But never kill a spider—it's said to be bad luck and cuts you off from money. If you meet a spider that looks dangerous or is bigger than you are, my recommendation is that you just fly away or run as fast as you can in the opposite direction.

A TRULY WISE WIZARD KNOWS WHEN THE TIME IS RIGHT TO FIGHT, AND WHEN IT'S BETTER TO AVOID CONFRONTATION.

Fairy Circle

Create a magic place in your garden that will attract fairies. Be warned, however, that it might get a little noisy. The Little People like to use fairy circles as meeting places at night, where they sing, dance, and make merry.

WHAT YOU NEED

- rake
- piece of rope or string, 6 to 10 feet (1.8 to 3 m) long
- small shovel or garden trowel
- red and white flowers to plant around the circle (*Impatiens wallerana* is a particularly good choice. If you plant them in full sun, you'll need to water them every day.)

- grass seed*
- straw
- water hose with spray nozzle or sprinkler

*Ryegrass (*Lolium*) grows quickly, but fescue (*Festuca*) grows well in shade. If you'd like a longer-lasting grass, ask for recommendations at your local garden center.

INSTRUCTIONS

1. Choose a semi-shady spot in your garden for the fairy circle, and use the rake to clear away leaves and brush.

2. Use the piece of rope to create the shape of a circle inside the raked area. You can make your fairy circle as big or as small as you like.

3. With the shovel, dig up any grass or weeds inside the rope outline, and put them in your compost heap. Break up any large chunks of dirt, and rake the area smooth.

4. Use the shovel or trowel to dig as many holes as you need around the perimeter of the circle for the flowers. The holes should be at least twice as big across as the potted sections of the flowers so the roots will have room to spread. Put a little mound of dirt at the bottom of each hole, too.

5. Gently remove the flowers from their pots and place them on the mounds. Then fill in the holes with loose soil. Fairies love the colors red and white, so try alternating the red and white blooms, or put them in another pattern that pleases you.

6. Following the package directions, sprinkle the grass seed over the rest of the dug-up, raked soil inside the circle. Sprinkle a thin layer of the straw over the seeded area.

7. Immediately after planting, give the flowers and the seeded area a good, long drink of water from a hose with a spray attachment, or set up a sprinkler to wet the area well. Keep the area moist for the next week or so. When you start to see green sprouts, it won't take long for the little people to be enjoying their new circle! Continue to water frequently enough to keep the flowers and grass in your fairy circle looking happy.

GIANT SNAILS and SLUGS:
More Completely Inappropriate Wizard's Familiars

If you spend time in a garden or park, I'm sure you'll spot the shiny trails of snails and slugs. I've never heard of a wizard with a snail or slug for a familiar, but I suppose there could always be a first time. If size interests you, the giant African land snail grows to 8 inches (20 cm) long. It's a big eater, though, and is quite a pest in tropical countries.

The banana slug comes from the Pacific Northwest, and this creature can grow to 10 inches long (25.4 cm) and a quarter-pound (112 g) in weight. Of course, you'd have to put a speed charm on it to get it to do anything quickly. Failing that, if you're ever in a tight spot and you need to get away fast, you can use your slug as a handy escape device. Just lob the gelatinous monster at your opponent, and by the time they finish cleaning off the goo, you'll be long gone!

MESSY, BUT EFFECTIVE.

GOOD MAGIC
Container Garden

If you'd like to grow a garden that's fairy-friendly and discourages evil trolls, here are the herbs and flowers to help you. By planting them in their own pots, you can move them around as you like. Some of these may already be growing in your backyard, so ask your parents or go out and see for yourself. Planting a little seed and helping it grow into new life is a very wizardly thing to do. After all, isn't it a miracle that a huge oak tree can grow out of a tiny acorn?

WHAT YOU NEED

- empty, clean flowerpots
- small rocks, gravel, or small pieces of broken crockery
- potting soil
- hand file
- trowel or kitchen spoon
- watering can filled with water

*Instead of seeds, buy a head of garlic, break it apart into individual garlic cloves, and plant each clove with the flat end pointing down, 1 to 2 inches (2.5 to 5 cm) deep and 3 inches (8 cm) apart. You can harvest it when the tops fall over and turn brown.

**This vine loves to climb, so put the pot next to a fence or trellis.

Seed packets of the following:
- angelica
- common thyme
- dill
- garlic*
- lesser periwinkle
- marigold
- moonflower**
- rosemary
- rue
- St. John's wort
- sweet marjoram
- thistle
- verbena

INSTRUCTIONS

1. Put a shallow layer of rocks, gravel, or crockery in the bottom of each pot to help drainage (figure 1).

2. Using the trowel or spoon, fill each pot with potting soil to 2 inches (5 cm) below the rim (figure 2).

3. Open one seed packet and thinly sprinkle the seeds on the top of the dirt, being careful not to crowd them. Repeat this process for all the plants, planting only one kind of plant in each pot.

4. Sprinkle a thin layer of dirt on top of the seeds, following the package directions on how deep the top layer should be.

5. Gently pat the soil in place with your hand, then water the seeds with the watering can (figure 3).

6. Put the pots in a sunny spot and keep the dirt moist, and soon your seeds will start to grow! Your magic garden plants will grow happily in their containers. Or, when your plants are several inches high, you can remove them from their pot and plant them in a sunny spot in your backyard.

EACH PLANT IN YOUR GOOD MAGIC CONTAINER GARDEN HAS ITS OWN SPECIAL QUALITIES.

ANGELICA (*Angelica archangelica*)
Angelica is the single most powerful plant against evildoing and bad magic. The plant is said to bloom on the May feast day of Saint Michael the Archangel, and tradition says every part of it protects against evil, especially the root. Its leaf stalks smell good, and they can be candied and eaten. Angelica can grow up to 4 feet (1.2 m) tall and likes a partially shaded spot. Keep the soil in its pot moist.

COMMON THYME (*Thymus vulgaris*)
Bees love thyme, as do fairies. It's a perennial herb and has tiny, fragrant leaves and masses of little light purple flowers. Thyme is great as a cooking spice, too.

Dill *(Anethum graveolens)*
Another delicious kitchen herb, dill was based on the old Saxon word meaning "to comfort." Since ancient times, its feathery fronds have been used to protect children from any bad ghosts roaming around at night.

Garlic *(Liliaceae)*
We all know vampires and evil ghosts hate garlic. People have eaten it through the centuries to stay healthy. The Egyptians used it when they took an oath, and Roman soldiers ate it for courage and strength. It's not as strong-tasting when it's cooked.

Lesser Periwinkle *(Vinca minor)*
This lovely, low-growing flower is a perennial, meaning it will come back year after year. It has dark green leaves, and white, deep purple, or blue blossoms, with five petals that grow in a pinwheel shape. Evil spirits can't stand periwinkle, especially when you cut some of it on a moonlit night.

Marigold *(Tagetes)*
Evil spirits that come out at night also hate light, so this gold-colored flower is excellent to keep them away. If you have tomato plants, plant marigolds nearby to help drive away bugs, too. Pick off the old flowers to keep the plant blooming.

Moonflower *(Ipomoea alba, Calonyction aculeatum)*
The moon plays such an important part in ancient myth and legend, it's fitting for a good magic garden to feature moonflowers. This fast-growing vine has big heart-shaped leaves and gorgeous white flowers that close during the day. At night the blossoms open up as big as salad plates and give off a heavenly clove-like smell. Soak the seeds overnight in water, then use a file to roughen up a spot on the outside of the seeds to make it easier for them to sprout. Be sure to put your moonflowers next to a pole, trellis, or fence they can climb.

Rosemary *(Rosmarinus officinalis)*
The Italians say that if you watch a rosemary bush long enough a fairy will creep out from underneath. Rosemary likes growing in pots. It has small evergreen needles, can grow to 3 or 4 feet (.9 to 1.2 m) high, and has tiny, lavender-colored flowers. If you brush against it or rub the tiny leaves, you'll unleash its powerful aroma. Cooks use rosemary leaves as a spice, too.

Rue *(Ruta graveolens)*
Also known as Herb-of-Grace, this gray-green plant has fernlike leaves and small yellow flowers. In olden times, villagers used rue to sprinkle water on themselves, to protect against evil brought by strangers. Maybe they thought the smell would discourage visitors!

St. John's Wort *(Hypericum perforatum)*
St. John's Wort is a low-growing herb with red-spotted, yellow flowers. Its scientific name comes from the Greek, meaning "over a phantom," because its smell is said to drive away evil spirits. On the Isle of Wight in Great Britain, if you walk on the herb at night, it is believed that a fairy horse will come and carry you off! Another member of the wort family is known as springwort, or blasting root. It's said to have the power to undo locks and open the entrance to hidden treasure, but if you try to pick the wild plant in the woods, it will run from you and hide!

Sweet Marjoram *(Origanum majorana)*
Bad witches hate marjoram, so plant lots of this fragrant herb in your garden to keep them away. It's also a delicious spice to use in cooking.

Thistle *(Cnicus benedictus)*
Hundreds of years ago, the French king Charlemagne prayed that God would help him relieve victims of the plague that was ravaging France. Legend says that God told Charlemagne to shoot an arrow into the air, and it would land on an herb to aid him. When the arrow fell to earth, it found a thistle.

Verbena *(Verbena officinalis)*
Verbena is also called vervain, and the Greeks named it "Sacred Herb." It was a holy plant to the Druids and they used a special ceremony to gather it. They waited until the rise of the Great Dog Star, Sirius A, when both the sun and moon were below the horizon. Pouring honey around the herb as an offering, they lifted it from the earth and waved it in the air using only their left hand. Hanging some verbena around your neck is also supposed to attract love!

Fairy Pavilion

Create a charming outdoor pavilion for the fairies that live in your garden or backyard. The directions that follow describe how to construct a basic frame for the pavilion. The leaves and flowers in your garden and the time of year you build the pavilion will determine how it is decorated. Don't be surprised if you wake up one morning and find the pavilion in pieces on the ground—some fairy parties can get quite wild.

WHAT YOU NEED

• garden clippers or shears
• pocket knife
• several feet (meters)
of raffia or twine

INSTRUCTIONS

1. First you must gather a lot of twigs. A walk in the woods or around your neighborhood will provide all the twigs you need. Choose those that have fallen to the ground; don't cut them from living trees. This makes fairies really angry. You need to gather at least four Y-shaped twigs to create the posts. These twigs should have a diameter of at least $1/2$ inch (1.3 cm). Then, gather several good handfuls of thinner, straight twigs. You can always trim long twigs into shorter twigs with your clippers or knife.

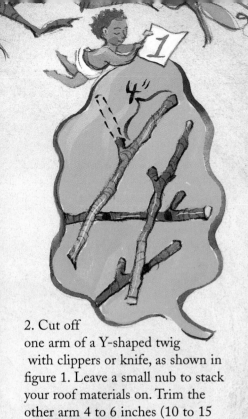

2. Cut off one arm of a Y-shaped twig with clippers or knife, as shown in figure 1. Leave a small nub to stack your roof materials on. Trim the other arm 4 to 6 inches (10 to 15 cm) long. Cut the other three Y-shaped twigs in the same way. Then, use clippers to trim the long, straight part of the four twigs to the same length. This will determine the height of your pavilion.

3. Use a pocket knife to sharpen the end of each twig you trimmed in step 2. Hold the twig in one hand and the knife in the other hand. Carve away bits of the twig, turning the twig as you work until you have a dull point on the end. Carve points on the other three twigs (figure 2).

4. Push the point of a twig into the ground. Use a second twig to create an eave crossing the angled arms. Decide where the arms will cross, and push the point of the second twig into the ground. Bind the crossed point with raffia or twine. This is the front of the pavilion. Create the back of the pavilion 8 to 12 inches (20.3 to 30.5 cm) away from the front.

5. Trim the smaller straight twigs to the length of your pavilion. Stack them along the eaves, using the small nubs to hold the first twig as you stack the twigs to the peak of the roof. This will provide a base for you to shingle the roof (figure 3).

6. Shingle the roof of the house with leaves, ferns, and decorative flowers. Tuck the stems of the leaves between the twigs; lay fern fronds on the roof lengthwise. You could also use sheets of bark gathered from fallen trees to shingle the house (figure 4).

7. Carpet the floor of the pavilion with leaves or bark. You could also use small stones to pave the floor, or use a large flat stone to create a front porch.

8. A good host provides a few extras: acorn caps for cups, a piece of soft moss for a bed, and a small stack of twig firewood stacked nearby.

A Fairy Primer

Elves, pixies, brownies, goblins, gnomes, leprechauns, dwarfs, and even ugly old trolls are all magical beings that only the most gifted of humans can see. Though most of them are Little People, some are human-sized and others giant. Whatever their size, they're all called fairies. Some fairies live in Fairyland and stay young forever. Other fairies live among us, including solitary fairies like the brownie, and the trooping fairies, who like to gather together for feasting and having a good time.

To see fairies, you have to be born with second sight (the ability to predict the future), or the fairies have to decide to show themselves to you. Otherwise, they're invisible. You can only see them between one eye-blink and the next, and if you try not to blink, you're trying too hard and that won't work, either. A fairy won't show itself if it thinks it will be doubted or mocked, and it might even be peeved enough to play tricks on you. Sometimes you can bribe fairies, with a gift and a little sweetened milk, to be nice to you. If a fairy likes you, it can help you with problems, or even give you money or gifts of its own. Dwarfs give presents that turn to gold, and when a brownie chooses a host family in Scotland, it will live in their house and do their housework at night!

Here are some tips for spotting the Little People. First, be very quiet! Leprechauns will disappear at the slightest disturbance. Perhaps they're afraid that you're after the famous pots of gold they bury at the ends of rainbows. If lockets or rings start disappearing from your room, you may have a dwarf close by; they're known to steal things, and they love gems and gold. If you hear the sound of digging and tunneling under your house, it's probably gnomes at their favorite pastime, searching for buried treasure. Plus, they like the dark.

There are a few places you might have good luck seeing fairies. Ireland, Wales, and Cornwall, in Great Britain, are absolutely crammed with them, along with Brittany, in France. Carry a four-leaf clover and watch for the official fairy tree, the hawthorn. Stay off the fairy paths called leys at Halloween, though, or the fairies may kidnap you. Fairyland time is supernatural, and two hours there could equal 200 years among humans.

Fairies love human babies, and they sometimes swap a fairy baby for a human baby to raise as their own. The substitute is called a changeling, and it tends to be ugly, with a big, hairy head. A changeling has a huge appetite but never grows any bigger, and it cries nonstop. If you think your baby brother or sister fits this description, wait a while. If your sibling grows, or starts to look better (and he or she probably will), you don't have a changeling at home, just a regular human.

Fairy Tambourine

The gentle music and sweet fragrance of this tambourine is said to be irresistible to even the shiest fairies. Use it with a kind heart to lure them from their hiding places.

INSTRUCTIONS

1. You can buy small grapevine wreaths at craft stores. But most fairies can tell homemade from store-bought, and they tend to be more receptive to things you make yourself. Simply wind grapevine, honeysuckle, or a similar woody vine around the soda bottle. Avoid any vines that look hairy: it could be poison ivy! Wind the vine around the bottle several times, occasionally threading it through the inner part of the wreath and back out again. Secure the circles of vine to each other by tying small lengths of floral wire in four or five places around the wreath.

2. Measure and cut four 24-inch (61 cm) lengths of ribbon.

3. Double a length of cut ribbon. Thread the folded end through the top loop of a jingle bell and pull through enough ribbon to loop around the wreath. Add the rest of the bells in this same way.

4. Thread the ends of the ribbon through the loop and tighten, pulling the bell close to the wreath. Tie a simple knot in the ribbon to secure the bell.

5. Measure and cut a 36-inch (92 cm) length of ribbon. Tie one end with a small knot to the wreath. Wind the ribbon all around the wreath form.

6. Decorate the wreath with fresh or dried herbs, leaves, berry sprigs, or dried or fresh flowers.

WHAT YOU NEED

- 2 feet (61 cm) of grapevine; honeysuckle, or other woody vine
- floral wire
- liter-sized soda bottle
- 4 yards (3.7 m) of ¼-inch-wide (3 mm) ribbon in one or more colors
- measuring tape
- scissors
- 4 jingle bells
- various fresh herbs and flowers

THE ART OF ANIMAL HUSBANDRY

Every wizard needs his own apothecary. I mean, I ask you, how can you cast a decent spell without eye of newt? If you're finding it hard to come by newt, unicorn horn, dragon's scales, or other essential ingredients, here are my most cherished recipes for making them, along with instructions for a handy apothecary carry-all kit. A wise wizard will also learn as much as possible about the natural and fabulous worlds, so he or she won't mistakenly slay a fearful, fiery dragon when all the poor beast wanted to do was toast some marshmallows!

The Absolutely Authoritative Field Guide to Fabulous Beasts in this section will help you avoid such mistakes by describing the appearance, behavior, and habitats of the best-known uncommon beasts.

WHETHER AT HOME OR
ON A VOYAGE, A WIZARD
SHOULD GET TO KNOW THE
LOCAL INHABITANTS.

ANIMALS CAN ALWAYS
TELL IF YOU LIKE THEM,
SO BE FRIENDLY!

THE ABSOLUTELY AUTHORITATIVE
Field Guide to Fabulous Beasts,

with a Guide to Pro-NUN-ci-a-tion

**Wizards need specific information to help them
in case they encounter a fabulous beast.
What does it look like? Where does it live? Is it dangerous?**

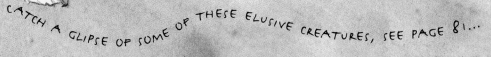

TO CATCH A GLIPSE OF SOME OF THESE ELUSIVE CREATURES, SEE PAGE 81...

Amphisbaena (am-fis-BEE-nuh)
This is a reptile with two dragonlike heads, one on its neck and one on its tail, which operate independently. One head can sleep while the other keeps watch. Has two clawed legs but, instead of running, the creature puts one head in the mouth of the other and rolls along like a hoop. Tends to be found in flatlands and lowlands, where it can pursue prey more easily.

Basilisk
(BASS-uh-lisk)
A monster whose glance can kill, it has a serpentlike body with two clawed feet, leathery wings, and a beaked, birdlike head. Produced when a toad or serpent hatches an egg laid. The safest way to kill it is to show it its own reflection in a mirror. Tends to be found in deserts, dungeons, and other dry places where there is no water to create a reflection.

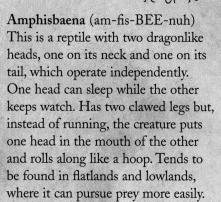

Griffin (GRIFF-un)
The offspring of an eagle and a lion, the griffin has a lion's powerful body, two back legs, and tufted tail, combined with the feathered head, huge wings, and clawed front legs of the eagle. It attacks large prey, such as elephants, tigers, and rhinos. Royal European families frequently include the griffin in their coats of arms. Its huge nests, made from small trees, are found in mountains, especially in the Russian Caucasus.

Hippocampus (hip-uh-KAMP-us)
A wild horse, green in color, it lives in herds on the sea floor, grazing on sea weeds and grasses. With the head and upper body of a horse, it has a full, flowing mane, clawed, webbed front feet, fins, and a long, fishlike tail. The creature is hard to spot because it is very shy. Herds are found off the coastlines of Europe, from Brittany in France, all the way north to Norway.

Kraken (KRAHK-un)
The most fearsome sea monster of all, the flesh-eating kraken is the mighty relative of the giant squid. Its horrible, beaked head is a terrifying sight, and its eight huge arms and two tremendous tentacles with barbed suckers are big enough to crush sailing ships. The kraken sometimes sleeps for a thousand years at a time before coming to the ocean surface to wreak havoc. In the past, kraken were frequently sighted off Norway, and today they are found miles beneath the ocean surface, in the world's deepest trenches and crevasses. It's best to avoid them altogether.

Manticore (MAN-tih-kore) With a human face on a lion's body, the manticore has triple rows of razor-like teeth. Its tail is like a scorpion's, with poison darts the creature can shoot at prey. Tends to hang around old ruins in the Middle East, though it's also fond of sleeping on carpets. If you're sightseeing and you see piles of bones lying around, or you hear a strange voice that sounds like a pipe or small trumpet, run! That's the manticore.

Merhorse (MER-horss)

A sea creature 40 to 100 feet (12 to 30 m) long, with a horse's head. Cousin to the hippocampus, it has smooth skin, big, beautiful eyes, and a flowing mane. It moves quickly, despite its huge size, and frequently has organized races with other merhorses in clearings on the ocean floor. Found near seaside amusement parks and betting parlors.

Ortus (OAR-tuhs)

A four-legged cousin of the phoenix, the ortus is a red-headed bird with a white face, black eyes, streaks of gold on its neck, white forepaws, and black hind paws. It periodically bursts into flame, but is reborn immediately. Usually found roosting in alchemists' laboratories.

Phoenix (FEE-nicks)

A symbol of rebirth and regeneration, the phoenix is a medium-sized bird with beautiful red and gold feathers and a lovely song. As it ages and comes near the end of its life, it builds a nest. At dawn, it sings to the rising sun, opens and closes its wings, and bursts into flame.

A newly created phoenix springs into life from the cooling ashes almost immediately. The phoenix is found all around the world, wherever there is new life and hope.

Questing Beast, The (KWEST-ing BEEST)

King Arthur is the most famous person ever to encounter the Questing Beast. He had stopped for a nap by a spring, but heard a noise as loud as 30 barking hounds. An animal leaped in front of Arthur. It had the body of a leopard, the back legs of a lion, the hooves of a deer, and a snake's head. It took off, with another king named Pellinore in hot pursuit. He never caught it, because that is its nature. You may see the Beast and desire it, but you will never catch it. Found near castles and hedgerows.

Triton (TRY-tun)

Half-human and half-fish, tritons have scaly torsos, fishlike tails, and a human upper body with claws and sharp teeth. They like having fun, blowing trumpets made from conch shells, and riding the waves. Sometimes they'll change their tails into legs so they can live among humans. They're found wherever the waves are good, so try Australia or Hawaii if you'd like to see the true inventors of bodysurfing.

Unicorn (YOU-nuh-korn)

A snow-white creature that looks like a horse, the unicorn has a single, beautifully spiraled horn growing from its forehead. Powder made from the horn will cure any poison, and a drinking cup made of the horn will change color if poison is put in it. The animal cannot be tamed, but if a young girl sits in the forest, it will come lay its head in her lap and go to sleep. Unicorns are found in forests all over the world.

Wyvern (WHY-vurn)

The wyvern looks a lot like a dragon, but it has only two legs and a barbed tail that it uses as a weapon. It has large leathery wings that it uses to fly, and a fanged, snakelike head. Wyverns like to have a good fight with a knight or two, so they can be found in populated areas attacking people and cities, hoping a defender will show up!

Yale (YALE)

Found near sacred temples in India, the yale was originally bred to guard holy places. A four-footed animal with hooves, it has dangerous curved tusks, and can point its two spiral horns in any direction. You can see it pictured in coats of arms. These days it can be found near any place you think of as holy, but it's hard to see. Most mysteries are.

Ziphius (ZIFF-ee-us)

Also known as the water-owl, the huge ziphius attacks ships at sea every chance it gets. Its huge head has a sharp, snapping beak and lidless eyes. The fishlike monster is larger than an average whale, and it can splinter a boat in seconds. It lives in all our major oceans, but the oceans are so big themselves, the chance is actually pretty small that you'll encounter the monster. Frankly, you don't want to.

Monsters of the Deep

If you're a wizard who likes to spend time at the beach or on the water, you're probably already familiar with sea monsters, or, as I understand it's more correct to call them these days, Physically Gifted Marine Presences.

Whatever we call them, they're still there. In these modern times, however, fewer people trust what they see, blaming hallucination, indigestion, or atmospheric effects. But some scientists, called cryptozoologists, suspect there's truth to the old stories, and investigate the existence of mythical creatures. We wizards could have told them so, if they'd just asked.

The ancient Greek poet Homer wrote a famous tale of sea journeys that describes a nightmarish, squidlike creature with fangs. I've found it most informative to read accounts from the days of sailing ships, when seafarers actually believed in these monsters—um, I mean presences.

When they came home from their ocean explorations, my Viking friends loved to hoist a few tankards and compete to tell the most stirring tale of their encounters with the Kraken, the legendary sea monsters said to live off the coast of Norway. In 1753 the Bishop of Bergen, Norway, described a monster "full of arms" big enough to crush a man-of-war sailing ship. The ten-armed giant squid does exist, and

it's 60 or 70 feet (18 to 21 m) long, longer than a city bus! There have even been reports of 100-foot (30 m) squid. With a cone-shaped head and eyes the size of a human head, the creature has a powerful, snapping, parrotlike beak strong enough to cut steel cable, and two powerful tentacles the size of fire hoses, with horrible, barbed suckers as big as dinner plates. Scientists suspect the creatures (named *Architeuthis* for "chief squid") live in one of the earth's deepest ocean floor trenches, in the South Pacific Ocean off New Zealand. They're searching for them in mini-subs at depths approaching 1,000 meters (3,280 feet).

But let's not forget the Loch Ness Monster, or Nessie, as she's fondly known. There are many legends about monsters in northern Scotland's lakes, and Nessie first appears in sixth-century accounts. Loch Ness is Britain's largest freshwater lake. It's cold, murky, and plunges to almost 1,000 feet (308 m) deep, with a huge underwater cavern near the bottom. If you were a sea monster, wouldn't that be a good place to hide? Eyewitnesses say that Nessie has a long, tapering neck that rises at least 6 feet (1.8 m) above the water, topped by a small, serpentlike head, with a huge hump. She's about 30 to 40 feet (9 to 12 m) long, with flippers, resembling the *Plesiosaurus* aquatic dinosaur, thought to be extinct. Or is it? So far, Nessie's evaded modern mini-sub explorers. Good for her, I say! EVEN A MONSTER NEEDS A LITTLE PRIVACY FROM TIME TO TIME.

Wizard's Apothecary

Every good wizard needs a wide range of apothecary items to make potions and jump-start spells. Here are directions for making a variety of hard-to-find supplies, in case your local stores are out of eye of newt or other essentials. To store them, start saving clean, empty spice bottles, jars, and other interesting glass bottles. To seal the bottles, you can buy corks in different sizes at a local craft store. It's my opinion, however, that dragon scales quickly lose their sizzle, so be sure to use them within one week. The Apothecary Carry-All on page 87 is great for storing small, dry items. You can easily tuck the box under your arm when you need to fly somewhere fast.

Narwhal Breath

(or Mermaid Gas Bubbles)

The narwhal is a rare Arctic sea animal with a long, straight tusk growing from its head. Did you also know that mermaids make bubbles just like you do in your own bath water? Whether they come from animal or mermaid, these potent potion additions make a satisfying pop when added to your cauldron. Gathering these seaborne treasures is a lost art, but you can make them for your own use if you have a steady hand and patience.

WHAT YOU NEED

• bubble wrap with large bubbles
• scissors (sharp embroidery scissors work best)

Instructions

1. Carefully cut between a row of bubbles on the bubble wrap. Cut an entire row.

2. Once you have a row separated from the main sheet, carefully cut around each bubble. Try to control yourself and not pinch every bubble as you go.

Baby Unicorn Horns

Take my word for it: Not a single, living unicorn was harmed in the preparation of this recipe. As you know, baby unicorns shed their horns every month for a few years until their adult horn grows in. But it is getting extremely hard to find these precious items in the wild. This version is a worthy substitute.

WHAT YOU NEED

• 2-ounce (56 g) block of silver-colored polymer clay
• cookie sheet covered with aluminum foil
• oven
• hot pads

INSTRUCTIONS

1. Knead the block of clay in your hands. Roll it into a ball and stretch it out. Repeat this action until the clay is warm and soft.

2. Pinch off a ball of clay the size of a small marble. Roll it into a skinny coil between the palms of your hands. Repeat this process until you have made three coils.

3. Hold the three coils together at one end, and gently push the end against a flat surface. Then twist the coils into a spiral, pulling them out to taper the end into a horn shape.

4. Make as many unicorn horns as you can from the block of clay.

5. Carefully place the horns on the cookie sheet. Bake them for about 20 minutes, according to the manufacturer's instructions on the package of polymer clay. Use hot pads to remove the cookie sheet from the oven. Let the horns cool completely.

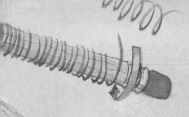

Dragon Heartstrings

A key ingredient in many potions related to courage, strength, and loyalty, dragon heartstrings are a mainstay of a wizard's supplies.

WHAT YOU NEED

• soft brass, copper, or other colored thin wire
• pencil
• wire cutters or scissors

INSTRUCTIONS

1. Measure and cut eight lengths of wire, each 18 inches (45.7 cm) long.

2. Tightly wind the wire around a pencil. Leave about 1/2 inch (1.3 cm) unwound. Repeat this process with the other seven lengths of wire.

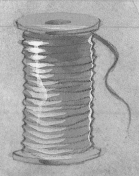

Red-Eyes of Newt

Eye of Newt is the salt and pepper of many potions, but who needs eyeballs rolling around and all over the place? Thread them on a string to store them: that way you can just pull off one eye at a time, or you can wear them as a power bracelet.

WHAT YOU NEED

• 2-ounce (56 g) block of red polymer clay
• 2-ounce (56 g) block of white polymer clay
• table knife
• 2 resealable sandwich bags
• tapestry needle
• oven
• cookie sheet covered with aluminum foil
• hot pads
• beading thread

INSTRUCTIONS

1. Cut the white block of clay in half. Store one half in a resealable bag for another project. Knead the white block of clay in your hands. Roll it into a ball and stretch it out. Repeat this action until the clay is warm and soft.

2. Pinch off small bits of clay and roll them into pea-sized balls. Set them aside.

3. Pinch off a bit of red clay. Store what you don't pinch off in a resealable bag for another project. Knead the red clay as described in step 1.

4. Make tiny little balls of red clay by rolling the clay between your thumb and forefinger. Set them aside.

5. Place a tiny red ball on a pea-sized white ball. Roll it between your thumb and forefinger just enough to flatten the red ball onto the white. This makes one red-eye of newt. Repeat with the other white balls.

6. Use a tapestry needle to pierce a hole in the red-eye of newt. Make a hole in one side, then pierce from the opposite side.

7. Carefully place the eyes on the cookie sheet and bake them for about 15 minutes according to the manufacturer's instructions on the package of polymer clay. Use hot pads to remove the cookie sheet from the oven. Let the eyes cool completely.

8. Cut a length of thread, thread it through the eye of the needle, and knot one end of the thread. Thread the eyes on the thread. Repeat until you have a long string of red-eyes of newt. If you want to wear the eyes as a bracelet, string the eyes on elastic bead thread.

Dragon Scales

Dragons are beasts of great magic and power, which makes this ingredient one of the rarest and most powerful you can add to your apothecary. Sometimes dragons shed their skins, scale by scale, to grow a new one.

WHAT YOU NEED

- dry, open pine cones
- garden shears or scissors
- metallic-colored acrylic paint
- small paintbrush
- newspaper

INSTRUCTIONS

1. Harvest dried pine cones that have fallen from the tree.

2. Use garden shears or scissors to cut the scales from the cones.

3. Work on a flat surface covered with newspaper. Use a small paintbrush to paint one side of a dragon scale. Let it dry, then paint the other side of the scale. Try painting the thick end of the scale a different color to indicate different kinds of dragon scales.

Apothecary Carry-All

Just the right size for dragon eggs. This shimmery box is perfect for storing the essential dry ingredients you need for making potions and other magic recipes.

WHAT YOU NEED

- empty paper egg carton
- acrylic paint in bright metallic colors
- paintbrush
- glass beads and flat marbles
- white craft glue

INSTRUCTIONS

1. Paint the egg carton inside and out with two or more colors. Let dry.

2. Glue on the beads and/or flat marbles for decoration. Let dry.

Toad Garden Castle

If you have a toad as a wizard's companion, here's an easy way to make a nice little castle for it to call its own. Garden toads eat lots of pests, so show your appreciation by giving them a place to hide from the hot sun.

WHAT YOU NEED

- medium-sized clay flowerpot
- 6 miniature clay flowerpots, 1 to 2 inches (2.5 to 5 cm) in diameter, with drainage holes in the bottom
- 2 twigs or wooden dowels, about 15 inches (38 cm) long, and thin enough to fit through drainage holes in pots
- photocopies of patterns on page 142
- carbon paper
- dried-up ballpoint pen or chopstick

- acrylic paint in white and other colors of your choice
- paintbrush
- trowel or large spoon
- small piece of heavyweight red or green plastic sheeting or vinyl
- fine-tip permanent marker
- scissors
- glue

INSTRUCTIONS

1. Wash and dry the flowerpots and set them aside.

2. Make photocopies of the patterns you'd like to transfer to your toad castle. Place a piece of carbon paper, with the carbon side down, on the outside of the large pot where you want a design to be. Lay the photocopied pattern on top of the carbon paper, and use the pen or chopstick to trace the design. You'll need to apply enough pressure so the carbon transfers the design to the flowerpot. Do this as many times as you'd like on all the pots.

3. First, paint the designs white and let them dry. Then, paint over the designs with the colored paint. This technique helps you get clear colors.

4. Find a shady spot under a bush in your yard or garden. Bury the big pot on its side, sinking it halfway in the dirt. Make sure the dirt inside is wet and crumbly, and put a few dead leaves and twigs inside.

5. Now you'll make the "towers" flanking the entrance to the castle. Sink the twigs or dowels 4 inches (10 cm) into the ground at the entrance to the pot, one on the right and one on the left. Holding one of the small flowerpots upside down over the dowel, thread the dowel through the drainage hole and lower the pot all the way down to the ground. Thread a second small pot over the dowel, but right side up,

so when it meets the first pot, they have bottom-to-bottom contact. Thread a third small pot over the dowel, with the pot upside down, until it has rim-to-rim contact with the pot underneath. There should still be about 2 inches (5 cm) of dowel protruding from the drainage hole of the third pot.

6. Repeat this process with the second dowel and the remaining three pots.

7. Now you'll make pennants to fly from the castle towers. On the plastic sheet or vinyl, use the marker to draw two isoceles triangles (which, as every sorceress worth her hat knows, has one short side and two that are longer and of equal length). Cut out the two triangles with the scissors. If you like, you can draw wizard symbols on the pennants with the marker.

8. Apply a line of glue along the shortest side of one of the triangles. Wrap the gluey end around one of the dowels sticking out of a flowerpot tower. Repeat the process to glue the second pennant to the other dowel.

9. Keep an eye on the castle. When you see that the dirt at the entrance is looking worn, you'll know that a toad has moved in. At twilight, you might catch a glimpse of Sir Toad waiting for an appetizing insect to fly by. Shazaam! Gulp! DINNER IS SERVED.

NEVERMORE...

ONCE UPON A MIDNIGHT DREARY:

Ravens, Cats, and Other Familiars

Do you think black cats are unlucky? Or that the raven is a symbol of bad tidings? Then you need to read more about what people in other ages and places thought. Their beliefs were very different and often much more positive.

The cat has always been viewed as the most magical of animals, for good or bad. Worshipped by ancient Egyptians who carried images of cats for luck, the animal was sacred to their cat-headed goddess Bast. Cats also symbolized freedom to the Romans, and the Greek goddess Hecate sometimes turned into a cat. Freyja, an important Norse goddess in the days before Christianity, was said to ride a chariot pulled by black cats.

As belief in evil witchcraft grew, people also thought evil spirits could take the form of small animals. Such animals, toads or especially cats, could become the

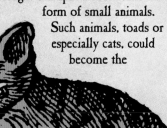

"familiars," or helpers to a witch. To this day, Americans and Canadians think a black cat crossing your path is unlucky, but British and Japanese people believe exactly the opposite. And how unlucky can a cat be, after all, if it's said to have nine lives?

If modern people continue to think ravens are only scavengers or bringers of bad news, maybe it's Edgar Allen Poe's fault. He's the famous writer of stories about the supernatural. His poem *The Raven* has the depressing creature continually croaking, "Nevermore!" I warned Edgar about the impression this would leave on readers, but he wouldn't listen to me. After all the help I gave him with his research...

The raven, or crow, is a devoted parent to its young, and it symbolized a happy marriage in Egypt. It was also sacred to messenger gods of the Celts and Greeks, and to Athena, the Greek goddess of wisdom. That's probably how the bird came to be associated with prophecy, shapeshifting, and transformation.

Maybe we've stumbled onto the clue to why some people don't like this bird. They may think that "the only good news is no news," or that "ignorance is bliss." All I can say is, I never knew a true wizard who wanted to remain ignorant!

chapter 5

THE BOOK ARTS

Reading books, writing books, actually making books—I've found it all to be great fun. (Good thing I remembered what the ancient Chinese taught me about printing books; I passed it on several hundred years later to my German friend Johann Gutenberg, but then he very unfairly got all the glory for making the first printed books! Ah well, *c'est la vie.*) Anyway, here are my instructions for creating a giant wizard's journal, a portable belt pouch notebook, a scroll, and a quill and ink to record your own wizardly thoughts and observations. If you want to keep your notes secret, I've thrown in a few recipes for invisible inks, plus a Runic alphabet that no one but another wizard can decipher. Or you can just hide everything in a book safe. My instructions for making it are on page 100.

Secret Journal

This simple book has the look of an old treasure, even though you just made it. The journal can be as large or as small as you wish. The size of the paper determines the size of the book. Fold in half a sheet of whatever kind of paper you want to use. This will make a group, or folio, of four pages. The book shown here is made with 12 sheets of 18 x 24-inch (46 x 61 cm) paper because I like having large pages—ideal for sketching pictures of dragons.

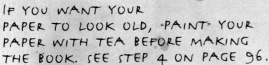

IF YOU WANT YOUR PAPER TO LOOK OLD, "PAINT" YOUR PAPER WITH TEA BEFORE MAKING THE BOOK. SEE STEP 4 ON PAGE 96.

WHAT YOU NEED

- 12 sheets of 18 x 24-inch (46 x 61 cm) paper*
- 2 pieces of corrugated cardboard, $12^{1}/_{4}$ x $18^{1}/_{4}$ inches (31 x 46 cm); recycled boxes work well
- table knife
- ruler or yardstick
- pencil
- scissors or craft knife
- awl or sharp nail
- large-eyed needle

- 2 yards (1.8 m) imitation leather cord, heavy thread, or string
- markers (optional)
- tracing paper
- 2 scraps of cardboard
- aluminum foil
- craft glue
- 1 yard (.9 m) thin ribbon in color of your choice

* copy paper and construction paper work well

INSTRUCTIONS

1. Fold the 18 x 24-inch (46 x 61 cm) paper so the short edges meet, one sheet at a time. Sharply crease each fold with the handle of your table knife (figure 1). Stack the folded sheets and set them aside.

2. Measure, mark, and cut two pieces of cardboard, each measuring $12^{1}/_{4}$ x $18^{1}/_{4}$ inches (31 x 46 cm).

3. Measure and mark a light pencil line 1¼ inches (3.2 cm) in on the long left-hand side of one cardboard sheet (figure 2). This will become your front cover. Use the handle of your table knife to score along the pencil line. Score lightly—you don't want to tear the cardboard.

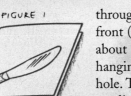

FIGURE 1

4. In the 1¼-inch-wide (3.2 cm) area of the front cover, measure and mark three centered points. Mark points 3, 9, and 15 inches (7.6, 23, 38 cm) from the top (figure 2).

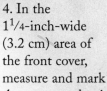

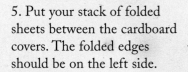

FIGURE 2

5. Put your stack of folded sheets between the cardboard covers. The folded edges should be on the left side.

6. Use an awl or a large, sharp nail to make a hole through the cardboard covers and pages. Work slowly and carefully. Don't push too hard or the pages will get out of line.

7. Thread your needle with 36 inches (0.9 m) of thread or cord.

8. Insert the needle from the back of the center hole, up through the pages, to the front (figure 3). Leave a tail about 6 inches (15 cm) long hanging from the center hole. Take your needle up to the top hole and sew down through the pages (figure 4). Now take your needle around the spine and insert it through the hole again (figure 5). Then, insert the needle up through the center hole and down to the bottom hole (figure 6). Insert the needle through the pages, around the spine, and back down through the pages (figure 7). Lastly, take the needle and cord back to the center hole and tie it tightly to the tail with a knot.

FIGURE 3

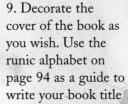

FIGURE 4

9. Decorate the cover of the book as you wish. Use the runic alphabet on page 94 as a guide to write your book title and your name on the cover. If you wish, you can use the markers to draw a design on the front. Or you can photocopy one of the many designs in this book and glue it to the front of the book.

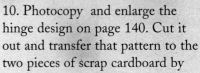

FIGURE 5

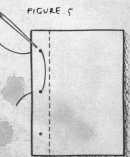

10. Photocopy and enlarge the hinge design on page 140. Cut it out and transfer that pattern to the two pieces of scrap cardboard by tracing around it. Then cut out the hinges, cover them with aluminum foil, and glue them to the front cover at the stitching points. Put something heavy on each hinge until the glue dries.

11. Use an awl or sharp nail to make a small hole centered on the right-hand edge of the front cover. Thread a length of ribbon through this hole. Repeat on the back cover. Tie the ribbons securely to keep the journal's contents away from prying eyes.

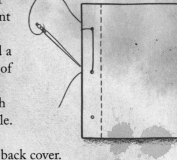

FIGURE 6

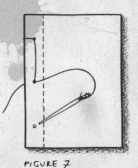

FIGURE 7

Celts, Druids, and the Morrighan

Many wizards and sorceresses will find Celts and Druids in their family tree, if they look back far enough. Although they disappeared long before even I was born—and I'm an old, old man—their reputation for magical power and wisdom endures to this day.

In ancient England, Ireland, Scotland, and Wales, the tribes known as the Celts honored their wise men and women, their seers and knowing ones, by calling them *wicce*, or witches. Female goddesses were revered, especially the Morrighan, a Sovereign Goddess and Warrior Witch. Morrighan means "Great Queen," and she was known to always travel fully armed and to appear as a black crow on battlefields, her cry as loud as the shouts of 10,000 warriors.

The oak tree was also sacred to the Celts, and their priests and sages were called Druids, or "people of the oak." Druid rituals were performed in sacred groves of trees and secret forest clearings. Mistletoe was the Druids' most sacred herb, and today we still traditionally kiss under the mistletoe that we use to decorate our homes at Christmas. The plant grows in oak trees, and was harvested by Druid priests with golden sickles, and caught on a white sheet as it fell. It was good luck to carry a sprig with you.

A few clues hint at the body of knowledge the Celts had. Some people think they built Stonehenge in England, a huge group of stones that line up precisely with the sun and constellations at the time of the summer solstice, the day of the year when the light of the sun lasts the longest. The Celts may also have constructed the many other huge standing stones and stone circles that can be found in Europe.

Emperor Julius Caesar wrote about the Celts, and the Roman historian Tacitus describes how Druids cast a paralyzing spell on invading Romans at the battle of Anglesey in the year 55 B.C. Who knows, perhaps the defending Celts had some help from the Morrighan and her fearsome battle cry that day, too. I like to think so.

ᚠ	ᛒ	ᛐ	ᚽ	ᚺ	ᛖ	ᛘ	ᚷ	ᚼ	ᚾ	ᛁ	ᚴ	ᛚ	ᛗ	ᛞ	ᚠ	ᚱ	ᛏ	ᚢ	ᚦ	ᛈ	ᚹ	ᛣ	ᚥ
A	B	C	D	E	F	G	H I&J	K	L	M	N O&P	Q	R	S	T	U	V	W	X	Y	Z

RUNIC Alphabet

The word rune means "mystery" or "secret" in ancient northern European languages. Runes were angular markings made by early English, German, and Scandinavian people beginning in the second or third centuries. The marks, carved in stone, metal, and wood, were used to record important information on monuments, to commemorate the dead, and to foretell the future. Each rune represented a different letter of the alphabet and symbolized a magical concept.

In Germanic tribes, the leader of the clan would pick three rune-carved sticks at random and throw them onto a white cloth. He would then interpret the matter at hand based on which runes he had chosen. For the Vikings, to speak the name of a rune or carve it on a sword was believed to call up the power of the god or nature spirit who commanded that rune.

To increase the magical properties of your journal, High speed chase broom, or amulet, you can paint or carve your name in runic letters.

Black Ink

From olden days to this very day, people who know how to write are often thought to have magical powers. I like to think about that when I write, and I like to make my own ink so that I can imagine that power going into the ink itself. The first time you write on paper using your quill pen and this ink, you may feel a curious tingle in your arm and hand. Wizards call this "writer's unblock."

MATERIALS AND TOOLS

- small bowl
- measuring cup
- liquid dish soap
- 10 nails or 2 pads of steel wool
- plastic food storage container
- white vinegar
- 4 tea bags (black tea)
- medium saucepan
- glass jar with lid
- white glue
- wooden spoon

INSTRUCTIONS

1. Pour $1/4$ cup (60 mL) of dish soap in the bowl and add 2 cups (473 mL) of water. Mix well. Soak the nails or steel wool in the soapy water for 30 minutes.

2. Place the clean nails or steel wool in a plastic food storage container and pour in enough vinegar to cover them. Soak for 48 hours.

3. Pour 1 cup (237 mL) of water in the saucepan and add the four tea bags. Bring to a boil and let the tea boil for 10 minutes. Let the water cool.

4. Pour $1/2$ cup (118 mL) of the tea water and $1/2$ cup (118 mL) of the nail/steel wool liquid into the glass jar. Mix in a little glue until the ink is thick enough to write with. The ink will turn black with age when you use it on paper.

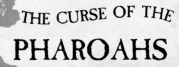

THE CURSE OF THE PHAROAHS

In November 1922, British explorer Howard Carter, and George Herbert, Earl of Carnarvon, uncovered the tomb of King Tutankhamen, which had lain hidden in the Valley of the Kings near Luxor, Egypt, for thousands of years. In addition to the pharoah's mummy in a solid gold coffin, the tomb contained riches beyond belief: jewels, chariots, and other treasures.

American novelist Marie Corelli wrote to the *New York Times* in March 1923, claiming she owned an old Arabic book that stated, "Death comes on wings to he who enters the tomb of a pharoah." She predicted the deaths of the tomb's discoverers. Only days after Corelli's letter appeared, Carnavaron died from pneumonia caused by an infected mosquito bite, and bad luck plagued people associated with artifacts from the tomb. Only coincidence, or something creepier?

YOU DECIDE.

Scroll

Early Egyptians and some Native Americans used scrolls to record many types of important events. Scrolls are an interesting way to capture a story, a process, or a recipe. There is something magic about unrolling the paper and discovering what has been written there.

MATERIALS AND TOOLS

- 2 wooden dowels, $^{1}/_{2}$ inch (1.3 cm) wide and 9 inches (22.9 cm) long
- 4 wooden beads, $^{1}/_{2}$ inch (1.3 cm) in diameter
- small saucepan
- 1 cup of water
- 1 tea bag
- 4 sheets of white paper, each $8^{1}/_{2}$ x 11 inches (21.6 x 27.9 cm)
- wax paper
- white craft glue
- 2 small paintbrushes
- iron (optional)
- 8 inches (20.3 cm) of ribbon

INSTRUCTIONS

1. Glue a wooden bead to each end of the two wooden dowels.

2. Bring the water to a boil and add the tea bag. Turn off the heat and let the tea steep for 10 minutes. You will use this tea to "age" the paper.

3. Use a dry paintbrush to paint a thin line of white glue down the 8-$^{1}/_{2}$-inch (21.6 cm) side of a sheet of paper. Overlap the edge of a second sheet of paper by $^{1}/_{4}$ inch (6 mm) or less. Press the seam firmly with your finger. Repeat until you have glued the four sheets together end to end.

4. Place the glued papers on a length of wax paper. Then, use the other paintbrush to "paint" the long edges of the paper with the steeped tea. Let the paper dry. If the paper curls too much when it has dried, you can flatten it with a hot iron.

5. Use the gluey paintbrush to apply a line of glue about 1-$^{1}/_{2}$ inches (3.8 cm) wide at one end of the paper strip. Wrap this end around one of the dowels and press it firmly with your fingers. Let it dry a bit and then repeat the process with the other end of the paper strip and the second dowel.

6. When both ends are dry, roll the dowels toward one another. Tie the scroll together with a length of ribbon for easy storage and transportation.

IN SEARCH OF KING ARTHUR, THE HOLY GRAIL, and the Mysteries of Glastonbury

Was King Arthur a real person? Hundreds of years ago, historians often embroidered the facts to suit popular taste, and storytellers gave heroes more magical powers with each retelling. But we wizards know that many myths have kernels of truth at their centers, and we also have the advantage of inside information!

Late at night, after a few tankards of mead, my good friend Merlin would loosen up and tell me stories about his days with Arthur. He was even responsible for Arthur's birth, you know. I loved Merlin, but he always was a bit of a windbag and emphasized his importance in stories of Arthur. But he was one of our most gifted wizards, no doubt about that.

Heroic, good, and wise, Arthur was one of Britain's greatest kings. Merlin used magic to help Arthur's father, King Uther Pendragon, attract Arthur's mother, Igraine. Arthur was born at Tintagel, a castle whose ruins still stand on the wild coast of Cornwall in England.

Arthur came to the kingship in the 5th century A.D., a dark time for Britain. Saxon raiders, who came to England as mercenaries for earlier British kings, were now taking territory for themselves, sacking every village in their path. Cities and towns emptied as people took to the hills to hide. In 12 glorious battles, including the Battle of Mount Badon, where he single-handedly killed 960 men, Arthur overcame rebels and invaders, and brought peace and stability to the country. Arthur

and his queen ruled from Camelot, which could have been the ancient Cadbury Castle in Somerset, England. Archaeologists have found the same type of expensive pottery (fit for a king!) at both Cadbury and Tintagel.

Arthur's very name is a clue to his existence. It's the Welsh form of the Roman name Artorius. In the fifth century, the British were still giving their children Roman names. In the sixth century, several men called Arthur suddenly appear in written history. Remember, people often name their children after great heroes.

Arthur assembled an order of knights, inspiring poets' stories of the Knights of the Round Table and their search for the Holy Grail.the miraculous cup used at the Last Supper. Arthur led his army to fight the Gauls in France, and disappeared from sight. Legend says he returned to fight his traitorous nephew Mordred in a battle at Cornwall. Badly wounded, Arthur was taken to Avalon, the enchanted Isle of the Apples, where he lies sleeping in a secret cave. One day, he will awaken and return to lead Britain to another golden age.

The mystical English town of Glastonbury may actually be the site of Avalon. Sacred to the Druids, Glastonbury also has the oldest Christian community in the British Isles. Glastonbury is crowned by the Tor, a terraced, volcanic rock formation 522 feet (159 m) high with church ruins at the top. The Celts believed the Tor was the home of the Fairy King, and mysterious bright lights

still appear in the sky above. According to legend, Joseph of Arimathea, who was either a disciple or kinsman of Jesus, visited Glastonbury. He planted his staff in the ground, where it grew into the still-living Glastonbury Thorn which blooms only at Christmas. Joseph also brought the Holy Grail. Legend says the Grail lies hidden at the bottom of Chalice Well, a radioactive natural spring said to have healing properties.

In 1191, the monks of Glastonbury Abbey announced they had found Arthur's grave. Guided by clues from a poem, they dug up a stone slab with Latin words that said, HIC JACET SEPULTUS INCLYTUS REX ARTURIUS IN INSULA AVALONIA, or, "Here lies buried the renowned King Arthur in the Isle of Avalon." Underneath, a coffin held the bones of a tall man who appeared to have been killed by a blow to the skull, along with smaller, possibly female bones. They reburied the remains. In 1278, King Edward I Longshanks opened the tomb, and an eyewitness described finding two painted caskets, one with bones of "great size." The relics disappeared in 1539, when King Henry VIII sacked the monasteries.

Were the bones really Arthur's, or does he sleep in Avalon waiting for our call? Whatever you believe, the stories of his greatness still inspire us.

Quill Pen

In many different cultures, feathers have long been used during mystical ceremonies. In fact, the ancient Greeks developed an elaborate system of divination based on feathers they found: the color, type of bird, and location of the found feather were all factors in interpreting the future. Since the quill was used as a pen in Europe for many centuries (in fact, the word "pen" comes from the Latin *penna*, meaning feather), it makes good magic sense to use a handmade quill pen for recording recipes for potions, writing down spells, and sending important messages to other wizards and sorceresses.

WHAT YOU NEED

- large flight feather with a sturdy barrel (the hollow, stemlike main shaft of the feather)
- cutting board
- small, sharp knife
- black ink (see page 95)

INSTRUCTIONS

The best feathers to use are the first flight feathers of swans and geese. These birds lose feathers every summer, so if you look carefully along the shores of lakes where these birds live, you may find one that's just right for a quill pen. Flight feathers have one narrow and one wide barb, whereas on other feathers the two sides are about the same. Place the feather in your hand as if you are going to write with it, and see how it feels. It should curve over your hand slightly.

1. Remove the barb from the lower end of the feather.

FIGURE 1

2. Place the feather on the cutting board, with the tip of the barrel pointing away from you. Use the knife to cut off the tip at a 45° angle (figure 1).

3. Cut a slit in the center of the barrel (figure 2). Stop cutting when the crack appears.

FIGURE 2

4. Turn the pen over and cut away a piece from the side opposite the slit (figure 3).

FIGURE 3

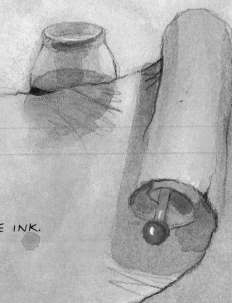

YOU WILL HAVE TO PRACTICE A BIT TO GET THE HANG OF USING A QUILL PEN & HANDMADE INK.

5. Now shape the "shoulders" of the pen on either side of the slit (figure 4).

FIGURE 4

6. Gently scrape away at the underside of the nib to make the surface flat and smooth.

FIGURE 5

7. With the underside of the nib downward and the nib pointing away from you, move the knife blade forward at a shallow angle to cut a small piece from the tip (figure 5).

8. Dip the nib in ink and begin writing!

Invisible Inks

There are several ways that you can make ink that goes on paper without a trace, but reappears when treated a certain way. Invisible ink is perfect for sending secret messages.

RECIPE #1
- **lemon juice**
- **toothpick**
- **iron**

INSTRUCTIONS

1. Write on a piece of a paper with lemon juice, applied with a toothpick. Let the juice dry.

2. To read the message, press the paper with a medium-hot iron. The paper may get a little smoky, but the message should appear fairly quickly.

RECIPE #2
- **1 teaspoon (5 g) cornstarch**
- **$1/4$ cup (60 mL) water**
- **small saucepan**
- **wooden spoon**
- **iodine**
- **sponge**

INSTRUCTIONS

1. In the saucepan, mix the cornstarch with the water.

2. Cook the mixture for two minutes, stirring a few times.

3. Let it cool, then use the liquid to write your message on paper.

4. Once dry, sponge the paper with a solution of iodine and water (10 drops in $1/4$ cup of water). Your writing will appear in a dark blue, and the paper will be a lighter blue.

RECIPE #3
- **1 teaspoon (5g) of a laundry detergent containing the ingredient that makes clothes "bright"**
- **fine-tipped paintbrush**
- **dark paper**
- **black light (one that emits long-wave radiation)**

INSTRUCTIONS

Laundry detergents that claim to brighten clothes contain a chemical that is activated by the sun's ultraviolet rays. In this recipe, we make an ink that shows up only under black light.

1. Mix 1 teaspoon (4 mL) of the detergent with $1/2$ teaspoon (2 mL) water. Too much water will weaken the effect; too little makes a paste that is visible on the paper.

2. Using a clean paintbrush, write your message on dark paper. Turn on the black light. Your message will appear on the paper. This will not work on white paper or under a regular light bulb.

Book Safe

Stow your wizard coins, ceremonial jewelry, or other valuables in this cutout book where it will be safe from prying eyes and sticky fingers. This clever book safe will fool the most devious criminal (or your little sister)! Choose a used book that will fit in with other books on your bookshelf. Don't choose a volume from an encyclopedia set: a single volume on the bookshelf might draw the attention of a would-be burglar.

WHAT YOU NEED

- used hardback book from a thrift store or garage sale (*Reader's Digest Condensed Books* have nice bindings)
- ruler with metal edge
- pencil
- piece of cardboard approximately the size of your book
- craft knife
- paper plate
- white craft glue
- small paintbrush
- wax paper
- heavy weight

INSTRUCTIONS

1. Measure the width and height of a page from the book you are using. Use these measurements to mark the piece of cardboard (figure 1).

2. Use the craft knife to trim the cardboard as needed. Safety tip: Work slowly and carefully when you use a craft knife. Keep your fingers out of the way of the knife's sharp blade. You may want to ask for adult help with this project.

3. Mark a rectangle or square in the center of the cardboard. The size is up to you, but be sure you leave at least 1¹/₂ inches (3.8 cm) all around the edge of the page. This will become your template for cutting the pages of the book.

4. Use the craft knife to carefully cut out the rectangle or square you have drawn. The rectangle you cut out is the template you will use to mark and cut the pages of the book (figure 2).

5. Open your book. Count 20 or 30 pages and leave those pages uncut to hide the cut portion.

6. Put your template on a right-hand page. Use a pencil to trace the template. Then, use a ruler and the craft knife to cut out this area (figure 3). Cut a few pages at a time. Do not try to cut too deeply. Remove the cut part of the pages. Repeat until you have cut all the pages.

FIGURE 3

FIGURE 4

FIGURE 1

FIGURE 2

7. Pour a small amount of white glue onto the paper plate. Brush the glue on the inside back cover of the book. Close the book to flatten the page.

8. Work with groups of about five pages: spread glue on the last page and press the group toward the back cover. Repeat until you have glued all of the cut pages together.

9. Put a sheet of wax paper between the cut and uncut pages, close the book, and put a heavy weight on top. Allow the book to dry overnight (figure 4).

10. Open the book to the cut pages, press open the uncut pages and the cover, being careful not to let the cut pages come apart.

11. Brush a thick coat of white glue along the outer edges of the cut pages along all three exposed sides. Brush a coat of glue on the four inner edges as well. The glue will dry clear. Put a sheet of wax paper between the cut and uncut pages, close the book, weight it, (figure 4) and allow it to dry.

12. Hide your valuables in the open area, put the book on the shelf, and rest assured that, as if by magic, your important wizard stuff is now invisible!

Chapter 6

THE ART OF ASTRONOMY

People have long believed that the positions and relationships of the sun, the moon, the stars, and the planets determine our characters and influence the course of our lives. (Many astrologers have enjoyed profitable careers as a result!) Twelve of the best-known constellations, or groups of stars, form the zodiac, and they carry names given to them in ancient times. Astrologers believe that your personality is determined by which zodiac zone the sun was in at the time you were born. Once you've matched your birth date with its zodiac sign, it's fun to compare astrological descriptions with what you know of yourself and your friends. (I've known more than one person who chose to believe the flattering parts, and disregarded the rest!)

SOMETIMES I'D LOOK AT THE SKIES AND WONDER

...IF THERE WERE OTHER WIZARDS
OUT THERE LIKE ME

Constellation Caster

A well-educated wizard should be able to identify the constellations in the night sky. To help you learn them, you can make these covers for your flashlight and illuminate the walls of your darkened chamber with the 12 zodiac constellations.

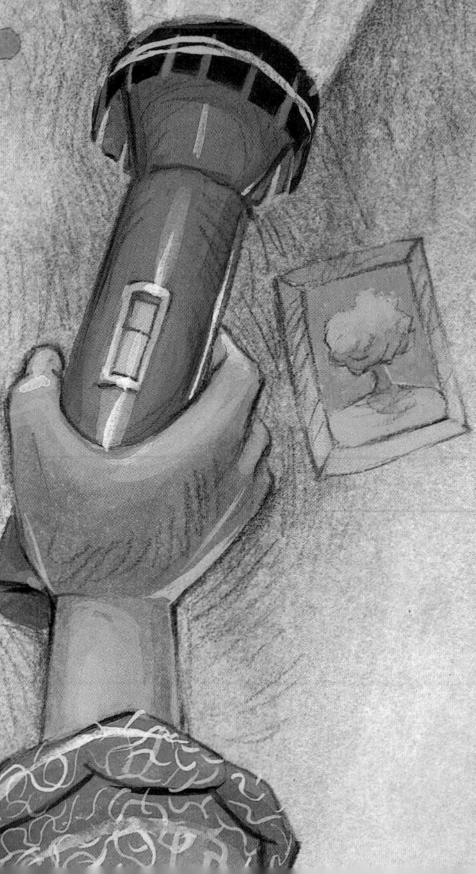

WHAT YOU NEED

- flashlight
- black construction paper
- pencil
- ruler
- compass
- scissors
- needle or push pins
- 5 to 6 rubber bands
- constellation patterns on pages 143 to 144

INSTRUCTIONS

1. Position your flashlight so that the lens is pressing on the black construction paper, and trace around the lens with the pencil. Put the flashlight aside. Then use the compass to draw a circle 1/2 inch (1.3 cm) larger around the one you have just traced. Repeat this as many times as you can on the sheet of paper.

2. Use the scissors to cut around the larger circles. To make tabs, cut the paper circles from the outside of the larger circle to the outline of the smaller circle, spaced about 1/2 inch (1.3 cm) apart all around the circle. Do this on all the circles you have traced. Then fold down the tabs.

3. Use the constellation patterns on pages 143 and 144 as a guide to prick holes in the circle with the needle or push pin.

4. Place the paper circle on the flashlight, fold down the tabs, and secure the paper circle with the rubber band.

5. If you're using the flashlight outside, turn it on and shine it against a wall of your house so you can match the constellation pattern to the stars in the heavens. In a darkened room, you can shine the constellation onto the ceiling.

What's Your Sign?

When our ancient cousins studied the circular (ecliptic) movement of the planets, they noticed the unmoving or fixed stars in the background. They used this background of fixed stars to identify the position of the planets. They divided the ecliptic path into 12 equal sectors. Each sector was named after the fixed-star group seen in that sector, such as Leo "the lion." The ancients called these sectors the *zodiac*, which in Greek means "little zoo."

Some people believe that the planets and their position on the day you are born represent certain "energies" that explain how you look and act, your likes and dislikes, even what type of job you'd be good at. Read the chart below and see if the description that goes with your sign of the zodiac sounds like a description of you. Then check out your best friend's sign...are you two a good fit? The chart also features the lucky colors, planets, gems, numbers, days of the week, flowers, trees, animals, birds, and metals that are said to go along with each sign. Is today your lucky day?

Aries the Ram
March 21 through April 20

Aries people are friendly, but also very determined and fearless, and they like to be the leader in activities and games. Sometimes they can't understand why their friends don't share all their interests. They are generous about sharing their belongings with friends, but have an explosive temper (which fortunately doesn't last too long). Arians tend to have broad shoulders, to walk fast, and to be accident-prone. They usually love to read, but can be a bit lazy about schoolwork. They tend to be explorers and pioneers in their chosen fields. Aries is most compatible with Leo or Sagittarius. *Red, Mars, ruby, 7, Tuesday, wild rose, holly, ram (or tiger or leopard), magpie, iron*

Taurus the Bull
April 21 through May 21

Taureans tend to have strong bodies and dark, wavy hair. They are calm and pleasant people, but sometimes very stubborn about getting their way. People born under this sign have a strong sense of fair play, more common sense than most, and good judgment. They are athletically and musically talented, and are good in school because they are good at focusing on getting the job done. Pastel colors (especially blue) and soft music make them feel serene. Taurus is most compatible with Virgo and Capricorn. *Blue, Venus, sapphire, 6, Friday, lily of the valley, apple tree, bull, dove, copper.*

Gemini the Twins
May 22 through June 21

Geminis are the original free spirits of the zodiac, and sometimes it seems like they can be in two places at once! They usually have sensitive, expressive hands with slim fingers. They make a lot of noise, have boundless physical energy, and are frequently late for appointments. Geminis are friendly, inquisitive, clever, have vivid imaginations, and they usually love to read and share ideas with others. Foreign languages come easily to them, but they need to learn to be patient and not give up on difficult tasks too quickly. Gemini is most compatible with Aquarius and Libra. *White and silver, Mercury, diamond, 5, Wednesday, snapdragon, elder, dog, parrot, quicksilver.*

Cancer the Crab
June 22 through July 23

Cancers are emotional, sentimental, and very sensitive people, gentle and patient with others.

They someimes feel lonely, and young Cancers often have imaginary playmates. They have very active imaginations, great powers of empathy for other people, and are frequently artists and creators. They can be good mimics, and they love a good joke. Cancers tend to be good at earning and saving money. In school, history is often one of their best subjects. Cancer is most compatible with Pisces and Scorpio. *Emerald green, Moon, emerald, 2, Monday, poppy, willow, otter or seal, seagull or owl, silver.*

Leo the Lion
July 24 through August 23

Leos are natural leaders and extroverts, and they can be lots of fun as long as they get their own way! Dignified, regal, and courageous, they're proud of their abilities. Sometimes Leos show off or act a little too exuberant for their own good. They have generous, warm hearts, and they like to show others how to do things. Leos are smart but they tend to rely on charm to get what they want, and usually have boyfriends or girlfriends before anyone else! Leo is most compatible with Aries and Sagittarius. *Gold, the Sun, amber and topaz, 4, Sunday, marigold or sunflower, palm or laurel, lion, eagle, gold.*

Virgo the Virgin
August 24 through September 23

Virgos are dependable, sincere, and able to work hard for long periods of time, so they're often the teacher's pet. They appreciate elegant things and have beautiful, intelligent eyes. Some Virgos are perfectionists and worrywarts, but their inborn critical abilities can bring them success in the arts, philosophy, or literature. Virgos love to read, remember almost everything, and often have hidden acting talent. They're choosy about what they eat, and value their privacy. Virgo is most compatible with Taurus and Capricorn. *Pale gold and yellow, Mercury, jade, 10, Wednesday, valerian, hazel, squirrel, parrot or magpie, platinum.*

Libra the Scales
September 24 through October 23

Kind-hearted Librans love fairness, and they hate to make decisions or judgments about people for fear they might make a mistake or hurt someone's feelings. They're good in debates and arguments, and often become scientists. Libras can be so charming with people, they may be in danger of getting their own way a bit too much! They often have dimples in their chins, love the color blue, and don't like watching violent movies or videos. Their rooms at home are usually neat and clean, and they have lots of boyfriends and girlfriends. Libra is most compatible with Aquarius and Gemini. *Blue and violet, Venus, opal, 8, Friday, violet, almond, hare, dove, copper.*

Scorpio the Scorpion
October 24 through November 22

Scorpios have powerful bodies, penetrating eyes, and a self-assured, magnetic quality that attracts people and inspires their loyalty. This is important, because some Scorpios can drive people away unless they control their temper tantrums and bluntness. When crossed, they won't rest until they've had their revenge. They like to find out what makes people tick without giving up their own privacy. They're good at solving mysteries and finding lost items, and they're often attracted to the mystical or forbidden. Even young Scorpios have lots of boyfriends and girlfriends. Scorpio is most compatible with Pisces and Cancer. *Red, Mars, ruby, 9, Tuesday, heather and chrysanthemum, holly, wolf and panther, eagle and vulture, iron.*

Sagittarius the Archer
November 23 through December 21

Sagittarians usually have open, cheerful faces with high, broad foreheads, and they can be dramatic and clumsy at the same time. They are idealistic, restless, curious, and love to be around people. Those born under this sign may find it hard to be tactful, to lie, or to tell a joke properly. They enjoy school, but can be spendthrifts unless they're careful. Many have strong spiritual yearnings, and find careers in religious or charitable work. Sagittarius is most compatible with Aries and Leo. *Orange, Jupiter, sapphire, 4, Thursday, carnation, mulberry tree, horse, eagle, tin.*

Capricorn the Goat
December 22 through January 20

Capricorns mature earlier than the other signs, and they value the wisdom and achievements of their elders. They respect authority and success, want it for themselves, and usually get it after a steady, determined climb. Many become diplomats and negotiators. Young Capricorns enjoy spending time at home. They like to organize their toys and belongings and to stick to set routines. Rather than being part of a large group, they tend to have a few special friends. You can depend on them to do their homework when they get home from school. Capricorns tend to be bashful around the opposite sex. Capricorn is most compatible with Taurus and Virgo. *Black, Saturn, onyx, 3, Saturday, nightshade and rue, pine and cypress, dog and elephant, owl, lead.*

Aquarius the Water Bearer
January 21 through February 19

Aquarians are one of the dreamiest signs of the zodiac, often having their heads lost in the clouds as they fantasize about the future. They tend to be taller than average, have straight, silky hair, and often droop their heads as if they are lost in thought. They are very curious about other people and have lots of friends. Quick thinkers, Aquarians also have excellent intuition about people, but they sometimes have bad memories about practical things, such as dates and times. They love being in nature, relish having their own freedom, and are quick to rebel against rules. Aquarians often become scientists or musicians. Aquarius is most compatible with Gemini and Libra. *Electric blue and green, Saturn and Uranus, garnet, 2, Saturday, snowdrop and foxglove, pine tree, dog, cuckoo, platinum.*

Pisces the Fish
February 20 through March 20

Pisceans combine the best points of the other 11 signs of the zodiac, but have their own special qualities, too. They are creative, artistic, impractical, love books and poetry, and don't care about getting or having money. They enjoy living in a fantasy world, and are often interested in astrology and magic. Pisceans tend to have hands and feet that are either small and dainty, or absolutely huge. They dislike routines, and are frequently most active at night while others sleep. They are very compassionate to the needy, and animals and children trust them. Pisces is most compatible with Cancer and Scorpio. *Purple, Jupiter and Neptune, 6, Thursday, heliotrope and carnation, willow and elm, sheep and ox, swan and stork, tin.*

CREATURES OF THE NIGHT!

Werewolves, Giant Ghost Dogs, and Vampire Bats

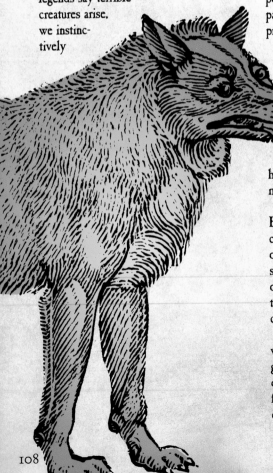

I will now tell some dark tales. My purpose is to warn you to be on your guard against all evil, whether it comes from outside or from within the human heart. But don't believe everything you hear, either. Quite frankly, I've heard some rather silly stories in my travels over the past several hundred years! You be the judge.

Since our earliest days, man has been afraid of the dark. When night comes and legends say terrible creatures arise, we instinctively draw together around the dim light of campfire or candle. I'll say the frightening names out loud: werewolves, giant phantom dogs, and vampire bats.

A wolf is a magnificent creature, but a wolf combined with a man's cunning and desires would be truly fearsome. The ancient Greeks believed that skilled sorcerers could shape-shift into werewolves by wearing a magic belt, using certain potions, or drinking water from a wolf's paw print. These were black arts, not to be practiced by good wizards.

There are many old stories of people who were bitten by a werewolf, condemning them at each full moon to change to half-man, half-animal, tormented by the knowledge of what they had become. Villagers discovered werewolves in their midst in households which always, mysteriously, had meat to eat.

How to protect against the monster? Believers say that silver buttons or bullets can stop a werewolf. If you throw a piece of iron or steel over the beast, its human self will appear immediately, bursting out of the pelt. Remember, people who are in the grip of a curse are to be pitied. Be compassionate, but be careful!

In Britain long ago, bad luck and death was believed to follow the appearance of giant black ghost dogs. In the countryside of East Anglia, England, night travelers feared meeting Black Shuck, a supernatural dog as big as a calf, with gleaming red eyes and an icy cold breath. Leaving no footprints, phantom dogs haunted graveyards and churchyards, and sometimes tried to break down the doors of houses. When my friend, the great detective Sherlock Holmes, investigated the case of the Hound of the Baskervilles, the frightened villagers at first believed the beast was a hound of hell! But as you consider this legend, think about your own dog's special gifts. How many times has your dog clearly sensed things that were invisible to you? Could it have seen a ghost? Too bad dogs can't talk, or rather, that we all can't speak their language.

The bat is our third well-known night creature, but we're mistaken to fear it. Gypsies think the bat is a benevolent creature, and carry bat bones in a small bag for luck. Yes, vampire bats (*Desmodus rotundus*) do exist, originating in Central and South America. No, they don't attack humans. They have bodies the size of an adult's thumb, and 8-inch (20.3 cm) wingspans. Making tiny cuts in the skin of sleeping animals, one bat drinks about two tablespoons (30 mL) of blood a day. Its saliva contains an anti clotting ingredient that may eventually be useful to doctors who treat stroke victims. But this should not be a surprise. As we wizards know, all things in the world have a reason for their existence, and it's up to us to be smart enough to figure out the gift they have to give. Including the gift of a little bat.

GREAT ALCHEMISTS OF THE PAST
and Their Search for the Stone

"Your money or your life!" I heard that line in a gangster movie and, in my experience, whether they're kings or commoners, many people want more gold and more time on this earth.

Centuries ago, alchemists searched for ways to make gold, or for substances to help them live forever. A few of them ended up in jail, imprisoned by greedy kings who wanted their secrets. Unhappily, a few blew themselves up with experiments gone wrong. But there were a few who became very rich and who've been seen hundreds of years after they supposedly died. My dear reader, didn't you ever wonder how I've lived more than 600 years myself? Think about it.

The alchemists were our earliest chemists. The Egyptians studied metals and gold refining, and the word alchemy may come from *al-khem*, the Arabic translation of Egyptian hieroglyphics that stood for "Egypt" and "black earth." These alchemical ideas spread through Europe. Alchemy was greatly respected during the Middle Ages and the Renaissance, and its successful practice required much study and the mastery of difficult arts. Alchemists deliberately wrote in hard-to-understand language. The word gibberish comes from the name of Jabir ibn Hayyan, an alchemist whose writings were impossible to understand!

If you've ever visited a modern laboratory, you'd recognize some of the equipment in an alchemist's workplace: furnaces, beakers, and glass phials that capture condensation from liquids. Other alchemical equipment was quite inventive, including baths of sand, iron filings, seawater, dew, and even dung—which provided heat from the decomposition of you-know-what.

Alchemists believed they had to perfect their souls in order to create perfect matter within God's kingdom. They believed that the final product of their work would be the Philosopher's Stone, a magical substance that made any substance perfect and turned any metal into gold. The stone would cure disease and give eternal life, and it symbolized the soul's perfection.

King Edward III hired the alchemist and mystic Raymond Lully to make gold. When Lully learned that the gold would not be used for spiritual purposes, he refused to continue and was jailed.

King James VI of Scotland hired an alchemist to make gold, but the experiment failed; and the same unlucky alchemist fell and broke his leg when he tried to use homemade wings to fly from the battlements of James's castle.

Legend says the greatest alchemical master was Hermes Trismegistus, an Egyptian king who reigned 3,226 years (!). One of the great founders of the magical arts, he was named after Hermes, god of alchemy. Trismegistus means "three times great." Legend says that when Alexander the Great invaded Egypt, he found the Emerald Tablet clutched in the hands of Hermes's mummy in the Great Pyramid of Gizeh. Legend said the tablet contained the magical secrets of the universe, and many alchemists hung a copy on their laboratory walls.

In the third century A.D., Maria Prophetissa wrote at length about the Emerald Tablet. A gifted alchemist, she also invented several useful vessels for distilling chemicals, including the glass beaker with a long, curved neck called the pelican retort, and the double boiler, which the French still call a bain-marie in her memory.

Nicholas Flamel was the most famous alchemist of the mid-1300s. Flamel made elixir from the Stone, became fabulously rich, and gave his fortune to charity. He wisely fled France after King Charles VI had him questioned about his sudden fortune. In 1761 a dozen people claimed they saw the 400-year-old alchemist and his wife at the Paris Opera, and to this day, there are still Flamel sightings around the world.

The Swiss Philippus Aureolus Theophrastus Bombastus von Hohenheim (1493-1541) renamed himself Paracelsus, and he became the greatest alchemist-physician of his time. Trained in medicine, he studied alchemy in Arabia and Egypt. Paracelsus was smelly, often rude, and his middle name inspired the word bombastic, which means pompous. He said physicians should help patients use their natural healing powers to get well, but he was so unpopular with other doctors that he had to flee town! After his death, he was seen in many places, and legend said he'd made himself immortal with the Stone.

109

Chapter 7

THE ART OF ALCHEMY

Even if you never succeed in making your own Philosopher's Stone, concocting things that ooze, bubble, smoke, or just plain smell bad is part of the fun of alchemy. But beware. Many a careless wizard has blasted himself clean out of his laboratory, so be careful to stick to the instructions in my *Magic Potion Cookbook* and don't add any extra ingredients. I've also included my recipe for all-important dragon's blood, in case you run short of local dragon donors.

LEARNING ALCHEMY WAS ALWAYS FUN FOR ME,
AS LONG AS NOTHING BLEW UP.

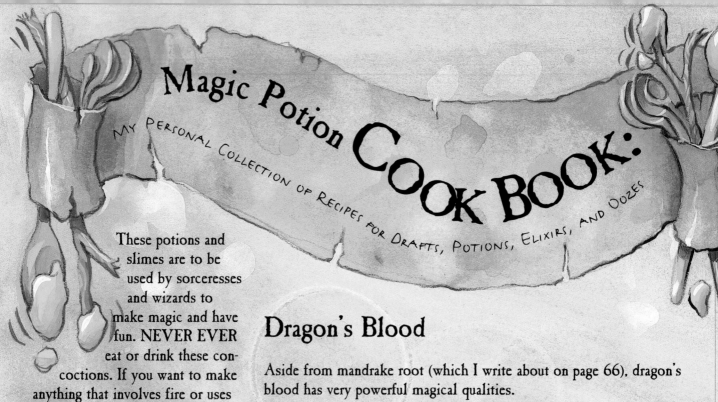

Magic Potion Cook Book:

My Personal Collection of Recipes for Drafts, Potions, Elixirs, and Oozes

These potions and slimes are to be used by sorceresses and wizards to make magic and have fun. NEVER EVER eat or drink these concoctions. If you want to make anything that involves fire or uses the kitchen stove, go find an adult wizard to help you (an adult non-wizard is also acceptable). I suggest that you start saving clean jars and bottles with interesting shapes. You can use them to mix your potions in, or to temporarily store them. Keep the original caps and lids to seal the bottles, or you can buy corks in different sizes at a craft store.

Dragon's Blood

Aside from mandrake root (which I write about on page 66), dragon's blood has very powerful magical qualities.

WHAT YOU NEED

- mixing bowl
- large spoon or spatula
- 1 cup (224 g) creamy peanut butter*
- 1 tablespoon (7g) powdered cocoa
- 1 quart (1 L) light corn syrup*
- $1/2$ cup (120 mL) non-sudsing soap
- 1 ounce (30 mL) red food coloring
- 15 to 17 drops blue food coloring
- $1/8$ to $1/4$ cup (30 to 60 mL) rubbing alcohol
- large jar or container with screw-on lid

*For thinner blood, use a bottle of dark corn syrup and 2 to 4 tablespoons (28 to 56 g) of peanut butter, plus the food colorings, soap, and alcohol.

INSTRUCTIONS

1. Put the peanut butter and cocoa in the mixing bowl and add the corn syrup until the concoction is runny, mixing everything well with the spoon.

2. Add the soap and food coloring, and mix well.

3. Add the rest of the corn syrup and the alcohol, and mix well. Pour the mixture into the jar, screw on the top, and shake well.

Kraken Slime

The giant, many-tentacled sea monster called the kraken is tough to wrestle if you want to collect some of its slime. The recipe below makes a very good substitute, and you can avoid the risk of being drowned at sea.

WHAT YOU NEED

• 17 ounces (510 mL) warm water
• clean quart jar with screw-on lid
• 1/8 cup (28 g) borax laundry booster
• small mixing bowl or cup
• tablespoon
• white craft glue
• green food coloring
• plastic food storage bag

INSTRUCTIONS

1. Put the warm water in the jar, and add the borax laundry booster. Screw on the lid, and shake until the borax dissolves. Allow to cool.

2. Measure 2 tablespoons (30 mL) of the white glue, putting it into the bowl. Add 3 tablespoons (45 mL) of water, and stir.

3. Add two or three drops of the green food coloring, and stir. Pour the mixture into the plastic food storage bag.

4. Measure 1 tablespoon (15 mL) of the cooled borax solution into the bag, then knead the bag with your hands to mix its contents. You now have authentic kraken slime.

Fizzing Phantom Potion

This is one of my favorite potions because anyone watching will be amazed that you can make plain water bubble.

WHAT YOU NEED

• glass jar or drinking glass
• bottle of white vinegar
• large platter or tray
• food coloring of your choice
• 1 tablespoon (14 g) baking soda in a bowl or jar
• water

INSTRUCTIONS

1. Fill the jar or glass half full with the vinegar. (If anyone asks, tell him it's just water). Place the jar on the platter.

2. With a dramatic flourish, add some drops of the food coloring to the glass while you intone, "I command you, phantom, to make my potion bubble!"

3. Pass your hands over the baking soda, pronouncing the same command, while secretly sprinkling the soda into the vinegar. Shazaam! A cascade of fizz will erupt.

4. If you want to further mystify your audience, empty the jar when it's finished fizzing, refill it with real water, then invite your friend to try to duplicate your magic.

Smoking Phoenix Ashes

The magical bird called the phoenix bursts into flame, turns to ash, and then is reborn from the ashes. Here's how to make a special ash that still smokes and glows when you touch it.

YOU MUST GET AN ADULT WIZARD TO HELP YOU WITH THIS RECIPE!!!

WHAT YOU NEED

• book of paper matches with cardboard cover
• metal pan
• scorchproof work surface
• extra match or lighter

INSTRUCTIONS

1. Go find a grown-up wizard or non-wizard to help you make the Phoenix Ashes. I don't care if you're a wizard in training, don't you dare go any further with this recipe until there's an adult standing there with you. I mean it. If you ignore this warning, I'll come back and turn you into a toad.

2. Tear off the scratchy strip from the matchbook (the spot where you normally strike a match to light it).

3. Open the matchbook and place it match side down in the metal pan, with the cardboard cover facing up. Make sure the pan is on a surface that won't scorch.

4. Carefully light the matchbook with the extra match or lighter, and let it burn until it burns itself out.

5. After the pan has cooled, rub your fingertip and thumb on the burned residue that's left on the pan. Rub your fingertip and thumb together, and you'll see your fingers smoking! (If you're in a dark room, they'll glow.)

Ghouly Green QUICKSAND

The most unique thing about quicksand is that it can't decide if it's a liquid or a solid. Here's how to make your own version of the deadly stuff. And if you happen to fall into quicksand during an adventure (and you don't have your broom to make an escape), the secret is to swim toward solid land using very, very slow movements.

WHAT YOU NEED

• newspaper
• mixing bowl
• 2 cups (448 g) dry cornstarch
• small cup or jar
• yellow and blue food coloring
• spoon
• 1 cup (237 mL) water
• jar with lid (optional)
• plastic wrap (optional)

INSTRUCTIONS

1. Spread the newspaper over your work surface and set the bowl on it. Put the cornstarch in the bowl.

2. Use the spoon to mix the yellow and blue food coloring in the cup until you have an acid-looking chartreuse color (it will take lots of yellow and very little blue). Mix the color into the cornstarch.

3. Slowly add the water to the colored cornstarch, using your hands to mix it thoroughly. When it feels liquid while you're mixing, but feels solid when you tap or press it, you've got quicksand! To keep it from drying out, seal it in a jar or put plastic wrap over it.

PRESTO, CHANGE-O
Chameleon Water

You'll cast a spell while pouring your magical Chameleon Water into a glass, then watch it turn dark blue/black. Pour it into another glass, and it's water again.

IT'S MAGIC!

WHAT YOU NEED

- 2$\frac{1}{2}$ cups (600 mL) water
- small saucepan
- 1 teaspoon (5 g) cornstarch
- mixing spoon
- large jar with a lid
- $\frac{1}{2}$ cup (120 mL) 3% hydrogen peroxide*
- 1 tablespoon (15 mL) white vinegar
- iodine
- eyedropper
- photographic fixer (also called hypo or sodium thiosulfate)**
- 3 clear drinking glasses with thick bottoms
- spoon or magic wand

*available at drugstores
**available at photography supply stores

INSTRUCTIONS

1. Put 1 cup (240 mL) of the water in the saucepan. Add the cornstarch, and heat on a stove over medium heat, stirring with the spoon, until the cornstarch dissolves. Add a second cup (240 mL) of water. Transfer the solution to the jar.

2. Put the fresh cornstarch solution in one of the glasses. Add the $\frac{1}{2}$ cup (120 mL) of hydrogen peroxide and $\frac{1}{2}$ cup (120 mL) of water, and use the eyedropper to add a few drops of the vinegar.

3. With the eyedropper, put a few drops of the iodine on the bottom of glass number two. Wash the eyedropper thoroughly, then use it to put two drops of hypo on the bottom of glass number three.

4. When you're ready to perform your magic, shout "Presto, Change-O!" and pour the contents of glass number one into glass number two (the one with iodine). The more dramatic you are, the better the spell is. The contents of glass number two will turn a bluish black.

5. Shout "Presto, Change-O!" again, and pour the contents of glass number two into glass number three, and stir with the spoon or magic wand. The liquid will become clear, but then will change back to bluish black in about 15 seconds.

CHAPTER 8

THE ART OF AMUSEMENT

Wizards really know how to throw a party, and here are some of my favorite recipes, table decorations, and party games. My *Spooky Food Cookbook* tells how to make everything from Crystal Candy to Crunchy Bat Wings, and you can serve it up on gilded feast platters or in my special dragon box. I'll also reveal how to make wizard toys, including my personal favorite, the revolving snake! You and your friends will also enjoy my *Really Useful Book of All-Good-Magic Spells, Cheering Charms, and Divination*. It's full of ways to tell fortunes and to attract good luck (would you believe tying a red ribbon to your underwear?).

ONE OF THE BEST THINGS ABOUT BEING A WIZARD
IS KNOWING SO MANY WAYS TO HAVE A GOOD TIME.

Great Horned Owl MASK

When I was in wizard school, we all loved a good party. Sometimes we would dress up as our own or a friend's familiar. Try this yourself and you'll wind up with a houseful of cats, rats, owls, and more. My faithful familiar Athena, a great horned owl, was the inspiration for this mask.

You can make this mask to represent any owl; just cut off the "horns" and color the mask to match your owl. Use an encyclopedia (or look on the Internet) for drawings of different owls. If your familiar is a cat or rat, simply change the ear shapes and add whiskers instead of a beak.

WHAT YOU NEED

- photocopy of mask and beak templates on page 142
- thin card stock (file folder, poster board)
- stapler or tape
- scissors
- craft knife (optional)
- coloring materials of choice (crayon, pencil, paint, markers)
- white craft glue
- 2 yards (1.8 m) ribbon
- small feathers (optional)

INSTRUCTIONS

1. Use a photocopier to enlarge the mask and beak templates on page 142 to fit your face. Staple or tape the pattern to thin card stock.

2. Use scissors to cut out the patterns. You can use scissors or a craft knife to cut out the eye holes.

3. Study your owl, and select colors to match its coloring. Color the mask as desired. Don't forget to color the beak pattern!

4. Fold the beak in half down the dotted line. Then, fold the tabs along the sides. Glue the tabs to the back of the mask.

5. Make small holes on either side of the mask, just about level with the eye holes.

6. Cut the ribbon into two equal pieces. Fold a length in half, slip the folded end through one of the small holes, and bring the ends through the loop. Tighten the loop carefully so you don't tear the mask. Repeat on the other side.

7. If you have small feathers, glue them to the mask as desired, and let dry.

Mold Garden
CENTERPIECE

Goblin Fingers, Troll Toenails, Ghost Toast, Eyeballs of Giant Blind Newt...if you want to delight (or gross out) your friends at a party, try creating a mold garden in a jar with these "ghoulish" ingredients. They can take turns guessing which is which. Assemble your centerpiece a couple of weeks before your special event so it has time to reach its maximum mold magnificence!

WHAT YOU NEED

- 5-gallon (19 L) glass jar with screw-on top, thoroughly washed and dried
- kitchen scissors
- paring knife
- toothpicks
- bookends or two other weights
- paper or cardboard
- fine-tip permanent marker

Any combination of the following ingredients:

- white sandwich bread (for Ghost Toast)
- peeled baby carrots (for Goblin Fingers)
- green grapes (for Eyeballs of Giant Blind Newt)
- unpeeled baking potatoes (for Troll Toenails)
- apples, oranges, and lemons (for Exploding Fruit)
- cheese (for Moon Chunks)
- pineapple chunks (for Bogeyman Brains)
- cooked spaghetti (for Dragon Innards)

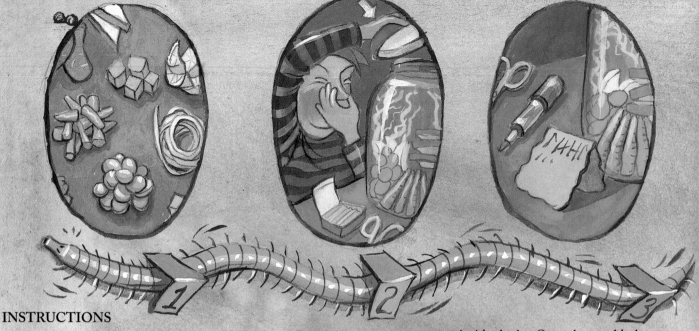

INSTRUCTIONS

1. Lay the glass jar on its side, or keep it upright if you want your Mold Garden to look more up-and-down.

2. Now you'll prepare the Mold Garden ingredients. See figure 1.

For Ghost Toast, trim the crust from the sandwich bread with the scissors, then cut the pieces of bread diagonally to make triangle shapes. Stack the triangles in two or three columns as high as you like, piercing them with the toothpicks, if necessary, to keep them upright.

For Goblin Fingers, lean the carrots against each other tepee-style, or lay them across each other log-cabin-style to build a little tower.

For the Eyeballs of Giant Blind Newt, peel the skins off the grapes and make piles of the grapes inside the jar. (You know the Giant Blind Newt is blind because the eyes have no pupils, right? It must live in dark underground caves all its life.)

For Troll Toenails, use the paring knife to cut the potato in half. Put the potato half flat side down, and cut from the top down, making half-moon slices that still have the peel on the edge. See how it forms a flat, wide toenail shape? Arrange the toenails as you like in the jar.

For Exploding Fruit, cut the apples, oranges, or lemons in slices crossways, working from top to bottom. Use toothpicks to stick the slices back together again, leaving a little space between them so it looks like the fruit has "exploded." Gently place the fruit assembly inside the jar. Mold should also grow nicely over the toothpicks, given enough time.

For Moon Chunks, use the knife to cut the cheese into cubes, and pile them inside the jar. We've often heard that the moon is made of cheese, and here's proof!

For Bogeyman Brains, make a stack of drained pineapple chunks inside the jar. Once they mold, they look very brainlike!

For Dragon Innards, arrange piles or coils of cooked spaghetti inside the jar. Consult an adult wizard about cooking the spaghetti if you need help.

3. Carefully place the jar in a warm, sunny place, without disturbing the contents, and brace the jar with the bookends or other weights to keep it from moving. Keep the jar open for a week or two to help the molds grow, then screw on the lid when things start to get a bit smelly (figure 2). Eventually, your Mold Garden will have an amazing variety of colors and textures.

4. Use the marker to write the names of all the items in your Mold Garden on the piece of paper or cardboard, and display it next to the jar (figure 3). After two or three weeks, the garden will be past its prime, and you can put the ingredients in your compost pile.

VENETIAN "GLASS"
Banquet Table Settings

The creation of Venetian glass was a closely guarded secret for many years. Delicately blown glass shapes of many colors flecked with gold were treasured by kings and queens. My own collection was small, but magical: when I uttered a certain spell, each guest's astrological symbol and color appeared in the glass. You can create your own versions of my table settings with paint and clear plastic party ware. You won't even need place cards at your next party—just ask your guests to find their astrological signs and then sit down!

WHAT YOU NEED

- 10-inch (25 cm) clear plastic plates
- clear plastic stemmed goblets
- clear plastic bowls (optional)
- photocopies of astrological symbols on page 42
- pencil
- sheet of newspaper
- gold and silver paint pens
- sea sponge (or other type of sponge)
- paper plates or foam meat trays
- acrylic paint in two bright, vibrant colors

INSTRUCTIONS

1. Photocopy the astrological symbols on page 42. Hold the sheets up to a sunny window and trace the symbols onto the back of the sheet. Since you will be painting the back side of the plates, you need to have the symbols reversed. You can use the reversed symbols as a guide by placing them under the plastic plates when you work or by using them as a reference.

2. Cover your work surface with the sheet of newspaper. Use a gold or silver paint pen to draw each guest's astrological symbol centered on the back side of a plate. Then, draw other astrological symbols around the edge of each plate. Allow the symbols to dry.

3. Dampen a sea sponge with water and squeeze out the excess.

4. Pour about 1 tablespoon (15 mL) of paint onto a paper plate or foam meat tray. Dip your sponge into the paint and then begin sponging color onto the back of the plate. Cover most, but not all of the surface. Repeat for the rest of the plates.

5. Repeat step 4 with a second color of paint. Try to cover all of the surface this time. Allow it to dry.

6. Use these directions to create bowls and goblets as well. Decorate the foot of the goblets as you would a plate. Add stripes, squiggles, or symbols of gold or silver up the stem and cup of the goblet. Leave at least 1/2 inch (1.3 cm) undecorated on the lip of the goblet.

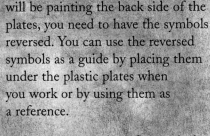

Banquets
OUT OF THIN AIR

There are certain mystics and holy men in the world who are famous for being able to produce solid objects out of thin air. These objects are called apports, and they include coins, candy, and gemstones. Some apports are much larger, including books, flowers, and live animals.

Some practitioners of Sufism, a philosophy with Eastern roots, are famous for the apports they can produce. So are Hindu swamis and holy men. Without apparent effort on their part, food, jewelry, and religious objects appear from nothing. Is it likely that there are tricksters among them, who cheat to create the illusion of magic? Yes. But there are also some mystics who have never been proven to be frauds. The Indian gentleman named Sai Baba can produce enormous quantities of apports. From sand on the ground or his closed fist, he can make entire banquets of food appear before you in serving dishes, plus desserts and candy. Very handy if you happen to be hungry, but I don't know if you can place your order with him beforehand!

Like most creative people, wizards have always been famous for being able to create something out of nothing. We all have some methods that we like better than others. Some of us don't mind sharing, but some of us like keeping our trade secrets to ourselves. I never could get Sai Baba to tell me how he does it.

Wizard Crackers

An English Christmas tradition, colorful paper "crackers" are filled with trinkets, paper hats and messages of good cheer. In other countries, crackers are stuffed with candy, party favors, and money. You have probably enjoyed them at birthday parties—pulling on both sides at once to make them pop. I'm sorry to say, these crackers do not snap, crackle, or pop, but they are delightful just the same. I have even used small ones to hold important messages, carried in the trusty talons of my owl, Athena.

WHAT YOU NEED

• 1 piece of corrugated cardboard, 5 x 7 inches (13 x 18 cm)
• paintbrush
• acrylic paint in color of your choice
• acrylic paint in metallic gold and silver
• rubber stamps in star and moon shapes
• 2 pieces of 8^1/2 x 11-inch (22 x 28 cm) colored paper in different colors
• scissors
• stapler and staples
• craft glue

INSTRUCTIONS

1. Paint the rippled side of the corrugated cardboard the color you want, and let it dry.

2. Use the rubber stamps and the silver and gold paint to decorate the cardboard, and let it dry.

3. Place the cardboard on your work surface with the painted side facing down. Place both sheets of colored paper on top of the cardboard, with the cardboard centered underneath. Trim the sheets of paper along the 11-inch sides.

4. Staple the paper to the cardboard at the four corners.

5. Place your gift or secret message in the center of the paper and roll up the cardboard/paper sandwich. Glue along the edge of the cardboard.

6. Cut the colored paper at both ends into ^{1}/4 inch (6 mm) strips to the edge of the cardboard. Carefully use the edge of the scissors to curl the paper ends.

spooky food
COOKBOOK

CRUNCHY
BAT WINGS

Although I have been a vegetarian for many, many years, during the first 100 years I heartily enjoyed chicken, buffalo, turkey, and fish of all kinds. Less appreciated as a delicacy is our friend the bat. The wings of this strange-looking mammal are slightly sweet, with just a hint of height and speed. If bats are not available in your part of the country, chicken wings are an acceptable substitute.

WHAT YOU NEED

Yield: 16 wings

• medium-size mixing bowl
• 1 cup (240 mL)water
• $\frac{1}{3}$ cup (80 mL) liquid smoke
• 2 tablespoons (30 mL) Worcestershire Sauce
• 3 tablespoons (45 g) dried parsley flakes
• $1\frac{1}{2}$ (7 g) teaspoons paprika
• $\frac{3}{4}$ (3 g) teaspoon garlic powder
• $\frac{3}{4}$ (3 g) teaspoon salt
• $\frac{3}{4}$ (3 g) teaspoon pepper
• 16 bat or chicken wings
• large resealable plastic bag
• shallow baking dish

INSTRUCTIONS

1. In the mixing bowl, combine the water, liquid smoke, Worcestershire sauce, parsley flakes, paprika, garlic powder, salt, and pepper.

2. Place the bat or chicken wings in the plastic bag and pour in the mixture. Seal the bag and turn over a few times to coat the wings in the marinade, making sure all the pieces are covered with the mixture.

3. Place the bag of wings in the refrigerator and marinate the wings for 1 to 2 hours, turning the bag once.

4. Remove the wings from the bag and place them in the baking dish. Throw the marinade away.

5. Bake the wings in a preheated 400° F (204° C) oven for 30 to 35 minutes. When they are cooked, turn on the broiler and brown the wings 3 to 5 minutes. Watch them carefully to make sure they don't burn!

6. Remove them from the oven with hot pads, and set them aside to cool to room temperature. (They are unlikely to fly away at this time.)

Petrified Tree
COOKIES

It goes without saying, you should never experiment with spells that could cause any living thing to turn to stone—be it an annoying friend, a barking dog, or a sneeze-making flower. If the urge to petrify comes over you, go ahead and make these tasty cookies instead. Add your favorite sweet ingredients, and see how spell-binding these treats can be.

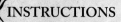

INSTRUCTIONS

1. Preheat the oven to 325° F (163° C) for a glass pan or 350° F (177° C) for an aluminum pan.

2. Place the butter or margarine in the pan, and put it in the oven for a few minutes to melt. Use the hot pad to remove the pan from the oven.

3. Sprinkle the cookie or graham cracker crumbs (or some of both) on top of the melted butter. (To make your own crumbs, place several cookie or graham crackes between two large sheets of wax paper and crush them with a rolling pin).

4. Pour the condensed milk evenly over the crumbs, trying not to disturb them.

5. Sprinkle on a layer of each of the following ingredients in this order:
• chopped raisins • chopped nuts • chocolate chips • granola

6. Place a piece of wax paper on top of the mixture, and press down all over with either the palm of your hand or the bottom of the measuring cup.

7. Peel off the wax paper. Put the pan in the oven and bake the cookies for 25 to 30 minutes until the top layer is lightly browned. Remove them from the oven.

8. Let the pan of cookies cool for 15 minutes, and then refrigerate for one hour.

9. Slice the chilled cookies into bars with the knife. Use the spatula to lift them out of the pan. I doubt there will be leftovers. But if there are, keep them loosely covered in the refrigerator.

WHAT YOU NEED

Yield: 1 dozen square cookies

• $^1/_4$ cup (60 g) butter or margarine
• 1 $^1/_2$ cups (215 g) cookie or graham cracker crumbs
• 6 ounces (180 mL) sweetened condensed milk
• 4 ounces (110 g) semisweet chocolate chips
(or butterscotch, or mint chocolate)
• 3 $^1/_2$ ounces (99 g) chopped raisins
• 4 ounces (110 g) shelled and chopped nuts or unsalted sunflower seeds
• 3 $^1/_2$ ounces (99 g) granola
• oven
• glass or aluminum baking dish, about 9 x 6 x 2 inches (23 x 15 x 5 cm)
• hot pad
• measuring cup
• wax paper
• rolling pin (optional)
• dull knife
• spatula

CRYSTAL Candy

Crystals are one of nature's best bits of magic. You can grow a crystal that looks real, but tastes good, too! You will have to exercise considerable patience when you use this recipe, but that's a quality well worth practicing!

WHAT YOU NEED

- 1 cup (200 g) granulated sugar
- ½ cup (120 mL) water
- medium saucepan
- food coloring
- 2 heatproof glass jars or small bowls with covers
- dull table knife

INSTRUCTIONS

1. Put the sugar into the pot. Add the water, but do not stir the mixture yet.

2. Let the mixture come to a boil and let it boil for 1 minute, still without stirring it.

3. While the mixture boils, add a few drops of food coloring.

4. Carefully pour the mixture into one or two glass jars or small bowls.

5. Cover the containers. Let them sit undisturbed for two weeks. (I told you that patience was required!) Slowly, as the water evaporates from the sugar mixture, crystals will begin to form. Observe the candy every day. When you see a crust forming on the surface, tap it with a dinner knife to break the crust so that the water can continue to evaporate. Do not, under any circumstance, shake, rattle, or roll the containers.

6. When the crystals are the size you want, use the dinner knife to separate the candy from the container. Then, reward your long suffering by eating a large piece before dinner.

Pumpkin Ice Cream Shake

WHAT YOU NEED

- 1 cup (340 g) chilled already-cooked pumpkin
- 3 cups (600 g) vanilla ice cream
- 1 cup (100 g) crushed ice
- ¼ cup (100 g) honey
- ¼ teaspoon (2 g) ground allspice
- ¼ teaspoon (2 g) cinnamon
- ¼ teaspoon (2 mL) vanilla extract
- blender
- 4 chilled 8-ounce (240 mL) glasses (stored in freezer for 1 hour)

INSTRUCTIONS

1. In a blender, combine the pumpkin, ice cream, crushed ice, and honey, and blend until smooth.

2. Add the allspice, cinnamon, and vanilla extract, and blend for 1 minute.

3. Pour the shake into the frosty glasses, and drink right away!

All Flavors
GUMDROPS

Raspberry, sour apple, Dead Sea salt.
Marshmallow, anchovy, chocolate malt.

Cook up six dozen in all kinds of
flavors. You may find several you
really will savor.

Here's what you need to make
lemon gumdrops, though my personal
favorite is gingered raindrops.

WHAT YOU NEED
(FOR LEMON GUMDROPS)

Yield: About 70 gumdrops
• 1 tablespoon butter
• 2 cups (400 g) granulated sugar
• $1/2$ cup (120 mL) water
• 1 box (4 packets) plain gelatin
• $1/2$ cup (120 mL) water
for dissolving gelatin
• juice of 1 lemon
• outermost part (zest)
of the rind of 1 orange
• 2 to 4 drops yellow food coloring
• $1/2$ cup (100 g) super-fine sugar
• baking pan, 8 x 8 inches
(20 x 20 cm)
• medium saucepan
• wooden spoon
• pastry brush
• small mixing
bowl
• oven
mitt
• knife
• scissors

INSTRUCTIONS

1. For those of you who like mucking about with anything sticky, this recipe is a dream come true…there's a reason why these candies are called gumdrops! However, the secret to a successful batch is a baking pan to which the gumdrops absolutely cannot stick. So start out by buttering the baking pan really well. Then set it aside.

2. Combine the sugar and $1/2$ cup (120 mL) of water in the medium saucepan. Bring the mixture to a boil over medium heat. Imagine the spoon is your magic wand, and stir, stir, stir! Every few minutes, wet the pastry brush in cold water and wash down the sides of the saucepan to prevent the sugar from crystallizing.

3. In the small mixing bowl, dissolve the gelatin in $1/2$ cup (120 mL) of water for five minutes.

4. Add the dissolved gelatin to the sugar mixture in the saucepan, and continue to boil for 15 minutes, stirring

attentively, being careful not to get splattered by the molten sugar syrup.

5. Add the lemon juice and the orange zest to the syrup and boil for five more minutes. Add the food coloring.

6. Slip on the oven mitt and very carefully pour the mixture into the buttered baking dish; then set it aside to harden for about three hours.

7. While you wait, do something useful: Help your mother clean the house; read two chapters from a book on astronomy; observe a bird in flight; or play with your younger brother or sister.

8. Time's up! Butter the knife, the scissors, and your fingers thoroughly (no licking is allowed—yet). Use the knife and/or the scissors to cut the gummy candy into pieces. Roll them into balls about the size of marbles, and then roll the balls in super-fine sugar. The balls will flatten out somewhat as they settle. If you keep the gumdrops in an airtight container, they will last for weeks.

Note: If you don't want to make 70 gumdrops of one flavor, you can make several flavors at one time. Cut a piece of cardboard into four strips as wide as the baking pan, and slide them into the pan to create dividers. When you get to step 5, divide the sugar syrup into three other small saucepans; add one quarter of the lemon juice and orange zest to one saucepan, and three different flavorings and food colorings to the others. Let the mixtures boil for five minutes. Then pour a different flavor into each of the divided areas.

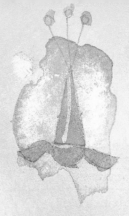

WIZARD FACT #155

If you want to create a lot of different flavors, such as root beer, banana, or bubble gum, you will need to buy extracts or oil flavorings. You can find extracts at the supermarket; oils are sold at some supermarkets and pharmacies, and from mail-order candy suppliers. Oils are twice as strong as extracts. Flavorings weaken with age, so don't buy too much at one time. For some unforgettable taste sensations, experiment with the following:

1/4 teaspoon (2 g) cayenne pepper

1/2 teaspoon (1mL) anchovy oil

1/2 teaspoon (2 g) garlic or onion powder

1/4 teaspoon (.5 mL) citric acid

1/2 teaspoon (2 mL) oil of cinnamon, peppermint, anise, or cloves

Throwing a
WIZARD'S PARTY

Wizards are a fun-loving bunch, and will use just about any occasion to have a party! Holidays, a doggy familar's birthday, a decent report card—they're all good reasons for friends to gather.

For a special party decoration, why not put up a Wizard's Tree? Buy a tabletop-sized tree or small, potted bush at your local garden center. Spray on canned "frost" and add twinkly lights. Have your guests blow up balloons in their personal astrological colors (see page 105), and supply them with pencils, colored paper, and scissors to make tree decorations (see patterns on page 42). Light carved mini-pumpkins with tiny flashlights, and get your parents' permission for Floating Magic Candles (page 49). Put the candles far away from guests or anything that might catch fire.

Drape your banquet table with a Celestial Sheet (page 60). Add extra tables set up for fortune-tellers with crystal balls, tasseography supplies, and palm reading instructions.

Brush or spray adhesive on netting, then sprinkle on glitter. When it's dry, tack the fabric up around the room for extra sparkle. If you have an ultraviolet light (available at hardware stores), you can have ghostly party guests! Blow up black balloons, paint on happy or scary ghost faces using glow-in-the dark paint, and attach to the ceiling with fishing line and tape. Turn off the regular lights, turn on the UV, and your phantoms will appear!

Embossed Dragon Box

Whether you use it to store gems, wizard money, or candy, this Dragon Box will be a magnificent addition to your chambers. A winged, fire-breathing dragon on the lid helps guard the treasures inside.

WHAT YOU NEED

- cigar box, $9^1/_2$ x 6 x $1^3/_4$ inches (24 x 15 x 4.4 cm)*
- large piece of cardboard
- scissors
- pencil
- white paper
- transfer paper or carbon paper
- photocopies of dragon patterns on page 143
- medium-point ballpoint pen
- ruler
- 2 disposable aluminum foil oven liners
- masking tape
- wooden chopstick
- thick craft glue
- silicone glue
- paper towels
- wooden clothespins
- heavy cardboard to line box, 16 x 20 inches (41 x 51 cm)
- $^1/_4$ yard (23 cm) of thin, decorative fabric
- cans or books for weights
- $^3/_{16}$ inch (4.8 mm) polystyrene board, 9 x 12 inches (23 x 30 cm)
- flat glass marbles
- extra-fine sandpaper
- paintbrush, 1 inch (2.5 cm) wide
- dark acrylic stain

INSTRUCTIONS

Transferring the Patterns

1. Cover your work area with the large piece of cardboard.

2. Use the scissors to cut the top from the cigar box along the hinge.

3. With the pencil and white paper, trace the outlines of the top and side panels of the cigar box (see figure 1).

4. When you go to a copy shop to photocopy the patterns, bring along the marked white paper so you can copy and enlarge the patterns to fit the traced outlines.

5. Use transfer or carbon paper to trace the dragon pattern onto the outline of the box top, and the other patterns onto the outline of the box front, back, and sides. Then cut out the paper panels.

6. Using the cigar box as a template, trace the outline in ballpoint pen of the box top, bottom, sides, and front and back panels onto the aluminum foil oven liners (see figure 2). Allow at least a 1-inch (2.5 cm) margin between the shapes.

7. Use the ruler and pen to draw a 1/2-inch (1.3 cm) border around each shape, (see figure 3). Press firmly. Cut out the shapes with the scissors, being careful of the sharp edges. Repeat this for each panel, except the bottom panel.

8. Tape the edges of the aluminum panels onto the cardboard-covered work surface.

9. Center the traced paper patterns on top of their matching aluminum panels, and tape them in place.

10. Pressing firmly through the paper, use the ballpoint pen to completely inscribe the pattern on each aluminum foil panel. Remove the paper and inscribe the outlines of the patterns even more deeply with the pen, but be careful not to tear the aluminum.

Embossing the Patterns

1. Now you'll emboss the patterns to give them depth. Use the chopstick to rub the background sections around the dragon and landscapes, jewel insets, and the areas inside the diamond and trapezoid shapes (see figure 4). Use the big end for the larger areas, and the small end for more detailed areas. The more firmly you press the chopstick, the deeper the background will be.

2. To raise the dragon figure above the surface of the aluminum even more, turn over the aluminum panel and lightly rub between the dragon's body and its wings, staying inside the lines of the pattern.

3. When you've finished embossing, fill the reverse side of the embossed areas with the heavy craft glue and let it dry overnight. This will keep the panels from being easily dented.

Attaching the Foil to the Box

1. Trim the corners from the bottom panel of aluminum foil, outside the outline of the tracing, as shown in figure 5.

2. Apply the silicone glue to the foil, using a thin bead on the edges around the bottom, and a heavier bead of glue inside the outline of the bottom (see figure 6).

3. Center the bottom of the cigar box on the aluminum panel and fold up the edges, as shown in figure 7. Smooth the aluminum onto the box, and wipe away any excess glue with a paper towel.

4. Trim the corners from the top panel with the dragon image, as you did in step one. Repeat the gluing and folding procedure to cover the cigar box lid with the dragon panel.

5. Trim the corners from the two side panels and the front and back panels. Fold back the bottom and side flaps on all the panels. Leave the top flap sticking up.

6. Working with one side panel at a time, quickly apply a bead of the silicone glue around all the edges, and in the center of the reverse side of the panel. Attach the panel to the box side, and fold the top flap over into the box. Press the panel and flap firmly into place, then use the clothespins to hold them until the glue sets. Repeat this process for the other three sides.

7. Use the chopstick to burnish, or firmly stroke, the corners so that the sides of the box look continuous.

Lining the Box

1. Use the ruler, pencil, and scissors to measure and cut a piece of the heavy cardboard big enough to fit the bottom of the box, but not too snugly.

2. Measure and cut a piece of the fabric 1 inch (2.5 cm) larger than the cardboard. For example, if the cardboard measures 8 x 10 inches (20 x 25 cm), the fabric should measure 9 x 11 inches (23 x 28 cm). Cut the corners from the fabric.

3. Quickly cover one side of the cardboard with a thin layer of the craft glue. Center the wrong side of the fabric over the gluey side of the cardboard, and press them together. Flip the piece over, and glue the edges of the fabric to the back of the cardboard. Run a thick bead of the glue all over the wrong side of the fabric-covered cardboard, and set it glue side down into the bottom of the box. Weight it down with the cans or books and let dry.

4. Cut pieces of cardboard that will fit inside the front and back of the box. Allow a ¼-inch (6 mm) clearance between the top of the cardboard pieces and the top edge of the box. Cut pieces of fabric, and glue them to the cardboard as you did above, holding them against the inside of the box with clothespins until the glue dries.

5. Make and attach side liner pieces for the box in the same way, but allow a ⅜-inch (9 mm) clearance between the edge of the liner and the top edge of the box.

6. Measure and cut out a piece of polystyrene foam that's ½ inch (1.3 cm) smaller than the box top. For example, if the box top measures 8 x 10 inches (20 x 25 cm), the foam will be 7½ x 9½ inches (19 x 24 cm).

7. Measure and cut a piece of fabric 1 inch (2.5 cm) larger than the foam piece. Cut the corners on a diagonal as you did for the box bottom. Apply glue to the foam piece, center it over the wrong side of the fabric, and press them together. Glue down the fabric edges. Weight down the piece and let dry.

Finishing the Box

1. Use the silicone glue to attach the flat marbles to their places on the sides of the embossed box.

2. Gently sand the box (except the bottom) with the sandpaper to give the aluminum "tooth," and sand down any rough seams.

3. Working on one side of the box at a time, use the paintbrush to apply the acrylic stain, making sure you get stain in all the outlines. (See figure 8).Wipe off the excess stain with paper towels while it's still wet, and wipe down the glass jewels so they're shiny. Allow that side to dry before you work on the next side. Use more coats of stain if you'd like your dragon box to look even older.

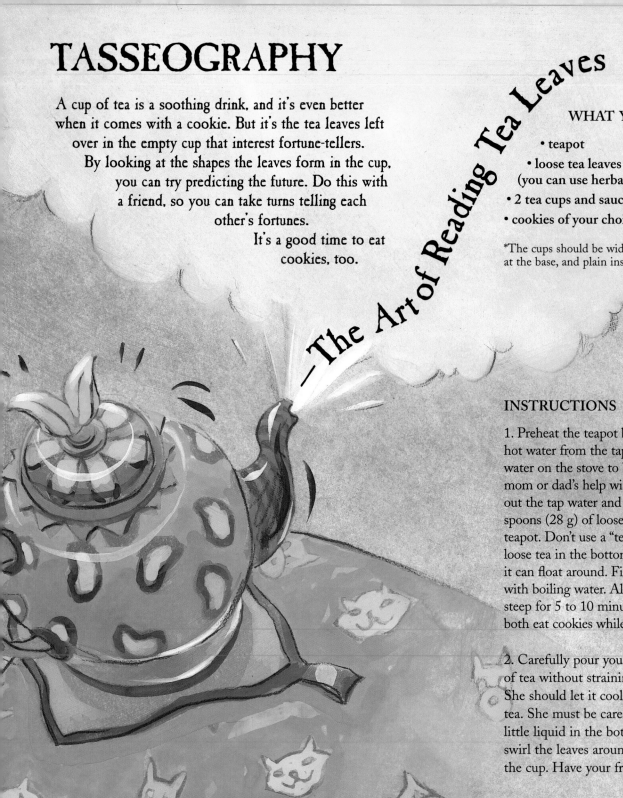

TASSEOGRAPHY

A cup of tea is a soothing drink, and it's even better when it comes with a cookie. But it's the tea leaves left over in the empty cup that interest fortune-tellers. By looking at the shapes the leaves form in the cup, you can try predicting the future. Do this with a friend, so you can take turns telling each other's fortunes.

It's a good time to eat cookies, too.

—The Art of Reading Tea Leaves

WHAT YOU NEED

- teapot
- loose tea leaves (you can use herbal mixes, too)
- 2 tea cups and saucers*
- cookies of your choice

*The cups should be wide at the rim, small at the base, and plain inside.

INSTRUCTIONS

1. Preheat the teapot by filling it with hot water from the tap. Put some water on the stove to boil (get your mom or dad's help with this). Pour out the tap water and put 2 tablespoons (28 g) of loose tea in the teapot. Don't use a "tea ball"; put the loose tea in the bottom of the pot so it can float around. Fill the teapot with boiling water. Allow the tea to steep for 5 to 10 minutes. You can both eat cookies while you're waiting.

2. Carefully pour your friend a cup of tea without straining the leaves. She should let it cool, then drink the tea. She must be careful to leave a little liquid in the bottom so she can swirl the leaves around the inside of the cup. Have your friend swirl the

leftover tea clockwise in the cup, three times. (If she's right-handed, she should use her left hand to do this. If she's left-handed, she should use her right hand to do this.) She should then carefully turn the cup upside down and place it on the saucer.

3. Turn the cup right side up and study the forms and locations of the tea leaves. The handle of the cup represents your friend, and any shapes close to the handle affect her directly. The rim of the cup is present time, and as you look deeper into the cup, you're looking further into her future.

4. In general, if the shapes the tea leaves form are clear, your friend is lucky. If the shapes are unclear, she may experience obstacles. Straight lines also mean definite plans, while a rippled line means uncertainty. Numbers in the top half of the cup represent hours or days, and numbers in the bottom half stand for longer periods of time, up to years. Any letters are the initials of people who will be important to her. There are many other symbols, and some are listed here.

5. When you've finished reading the leaves, now it's your turn to hear what your friend sees in your future!

Balloon = troubles are ending
Bell = good news
Bird = good or bad news
Boat = travel
Book = wisdom
Castle = money!
Cat = a girlfriend is involved
Chair = a guest
Circle = frustration
Cloud = doubt
Clover = good luck!
Cross = bad luck!
Dog = a good friend
Elephant = a friend's advice
Flag = a warning
Flower = love and honor

Garden = prosperity
Gate = an opportunity
Heart = love
Horseshoe = good luck
Key = an opportunity,
or discovery of a secret
Knife = a misunderstanding
Man = a visitor
Scissors = an argument at home
Snake = an enemy
Square = protection
Star = success
Tree = a goal will be
successfully achieved
Triangle = good luck
Wheel = money

133

Chromatrope

Years before motion pictures became widely available, wizards knew about (but weren't sharing) the scientific phenomenon called Persistence of Vision. The wizard of Menlo Park, New Jersey—Thomas Edison—and his associates let slip the secret, and motion pictures soon became standard entertainment for everyone. Though you can't replicate intergalactic battle scenes with this simple toy, you will see an amazing combination of the two patterns you place on your disc.

WHAT YOU NEED

- photocopy of designs on page 143
- scissors
- thin, cardboard or manilla folder
- craft glue
- pencil
- colored pencils, markers, crayons*
- 40 inches (1.1 m) of thin, strong string

INSTRUCTIONS

1. Photocopy two of the designs on page 143.

2. Cut them out, and glue the two circles to the cardboard or manilla folder. Cut them out, and glue them together, back to back. Color the designs as desired.

3. Make two marks, 3/4 inches (2 cm) apart, in the center of the disc. Use a sharp pencil to make small holes in the disc where you have made your marks.

4. Thread the thin string through the two holes. Tie the ends together in a knot.

4. Wind up the toy by swinging it over and over in the middle of the two loops with your hands, holding the ends of the string with your fingers. Make sure that the disc is centered on the string. When you pull your hands apart, the disc will spin back and rewind itself. You should be able to see the patterns and colors on both sides as the disc spins.

*Note: Don't use more than four colors to color the designs: too many colors make the phenomenon difficult to see. You can draw your own designs as well—just don't make them too complex. Simple shapes and colors work well.

Spinning Serpent

Not everyone knows the simple fact that heat rises. Wizards through the ages have amazed and confounded the uninitiated with this simple, spinning serpent. Be sure to hold your hand exceptionally still, mutter the appropriate spell, and you'll have your friends asking: "How ever does he do that?"

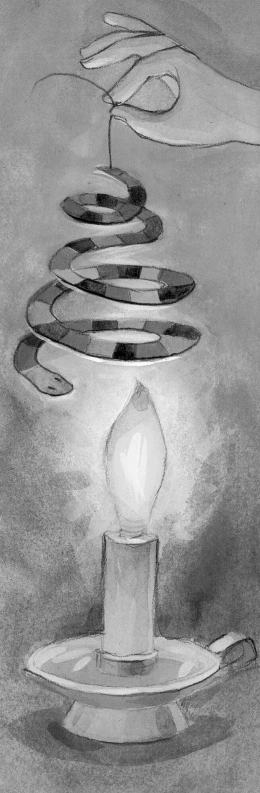

WHAT YOU NEED

- photocopy of snake template on page 142
  - construction paper
  - stapler
  - scissors
  - colored pencils, markers, crayons (optional)
- sewing needle
- sewing thread
- table lamp with electric light bulb (remove the lamp shade if you wish)

INSTRUCTIONS

1. Photocopy the pattern on page 142.

2. Staple the pattern you have photocopied pattern onto construction paper.

3. Use scissors to cut the spiral pattern. Work slowly and carefully, and cut the spiral smoothly.

4. Color the snake pattern if you wish. Create a coral snake brightly banded in red, yellow, and black, or a diamond-back rattler.

5. Thread the needle with a 12-inch (30.5 cm) length of thread, and knot the end of the thread. Use the needle to poke a hole in the end of the serpent's tail, and pull the thread through.

6. Suspend the serpent by the thread a few inches above an electric light bulb. When you turn on the light, the serpent will slowly rotate as the heat from the bulb rises.

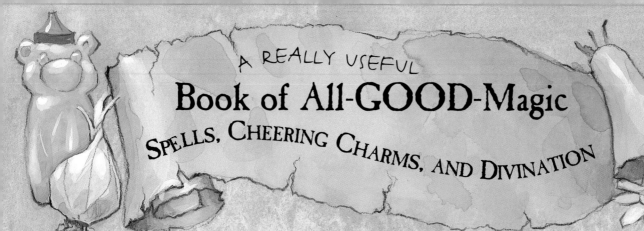

Book of All-GOOD-Magic

Spells, Cheering Charms, and Divination

Spells and charms can be words (Abracadabra!), things (a four-leaf clover), or a special ritual, such as always wearing your lucky red underwear the day of a ball game. Divination is another word for fortune-telling, and there are dozens of ways to try to see into the future, including palmistry and reading tea leaves.

When is a good time for a spell, and how do you cast a spell?
The first day of the month is a good time for spells, because it represents hope and a fresh start. For good luck on that day, some people also say the word "rabbits" before they say anything else! Or when they wake up, they say "hares" three times before they get out of bed.

Times change. Depending on what century it was, wizards used to accompany their spells with a

little burning incense and gifts of honey, butter, dates, garlic, wool, or precious stones (the last item is still welcome today).

What are some good charms?
Iron from a meteor is considered a powerful charm because it also comes from the heavens. So, the next time one falls in your backyard, let it cool, then dig it up with a shovel and make a wish on it.

Legend says keys can attract magic and protect against evil. Find one you like at a flea market or junk store, take it home and clean it, and keep it in your room. If you find several keys you like, string them from a bent coat hanger to make a lucky wind chime.

Changing Spells and Word Charms
Shazaam! Alakazam! Open, Sesame! Presto, Change-O! Abracadabra!

Abracadabra is one of a wizard's most important words of power. In A.D. 208, the doctor to the Roman emperor Septimius Severus wrote that the word was used as a charm to cure fever. It was written in the form shown

here, to encourage the fever to shrink in the same way. You can also write it with the point up, to encourage something to grow.

```
A B R A C A D A B R A
A B R A C A D A B R
A B R A C A D A B
A B R A C A D A
A B R A C A D
A B R A C A
A B R A C
A B R A
A B R
A B
A
```

Word charms often have words that are built up to increase their power, or shrunk to reduce the power of something else, such as an enemy or an illness. Try making up some names of increasing power yourself! "*Ray Raymond Raymondo Raymondotondo,*" for example, or "*Al Ali Alice Alicia Allegria.*"

Tying the Knot with Counting Spells
Did you know that the Russian and Hebrew words for magician translate

as "*knot tier*"? In the ancient Aramaic language, the same word is used for knot and charm. You can use counting spells to either attract or get rid of something. Take a string, a scarf (green is a good color), or anything else you can tie, and tie knots in it to represent what's on your mind. If there's a boy in your class you like, tie a knot or two one night when there's a full moon, and he may grow to like you, too. If you're worried about a problem, tie a knot to represent your worry, and bury the string in the backyard to get rid of it. (Better not do this spell with one of your mother's good scarves!)

Spells for Healing

This spell was used by the Teutons in the tenth century to ask the god Woden's help in healing an injury.

Then charmed Woden
As well he knew how
For bone sprain
For blood sprain
Bone to bone
Blood to blood
Limb to limbs
As though they were glued.

Spells For Love and Friendship

The Romany Gypsies thought fairies sometimes tied knots in the boughs of willow trees, and that the knots had powerful love magic. If you like someone and you find such a knot, sleep with it under your pillow to bind that person to you. If you want to undo the attraction, untie the knot.

Want to know the name of your future romantic partner? Write the letters of the alphabet on squares of cardboard, one letter per piece. Float them face down in a bowl of water overnight. When you wake up, the letters that have turned face up will be the initials of the special person in your future!

If you and a friend both carry a little bag with some whole cloves sewn inside, you'll always be friends.

Spells For Luck

If you find a coin with your birth year printed on it, keep it and carry it with you. It's good luck. It's also lucky to put a penny in your penny loafers, if you have a pair.

If you find a horseshoe, good luck is coming to you, and you get a year of luck for each nail that is still in the shoe. Nail the shoe over the door with the points up to "catch" and hold good luck in the house.

To get rid of bad luck, put sharp or pointed things, such as nails, inside a bottle, filling it halfway. Bury the bottle, and don't ever dig it up.

Four-leaf clovers are very lucky. The first leaf to the left of the stem attracts fame, the second money, the third love, and the fourth good health.

Bugs are good! It's lucky to have a bee in your house. It brings wisdom, happiness, and prosperity. Small

spiders in the house are good luck, too, and never kill a ladybug that flies inside or you'll bring bad luck.

Spells for Making Wishes Come True

If you see a falling star at night, say your wish three times very quickly before the star fades from view. Your birthday is a very good day to make a wish.

Write a wish on a bay leaf (write small, and use a fine-point pen). Carefully bury the leaf, and wait for your wish to come true. Add a marigold blossom from your Good Magic Container Garden (page 73) for more power.

A sprig of lavender put under your pillow at night will help your dreams come true. (This could work two ways, when you think about it. Hopefully, you'll have only good dreams!)

There's a reason genies traditionally come from a bottle! Write a wish on a piece of paper, seal it in a bottle with a cork or stopper, and float the bottle out to sea.

Spells for Protection

Have you ever felt like somebody was giving you the "evil eye"?

Try carrying an eye yourself (see the Red-Eyes of Newt instructions on page 86). Carrying bells, something made of brass, garlic (phew!), or tying a red ribbon to your underwear are also recommended.

Your Future is at Hand, or,

How to Read Palms

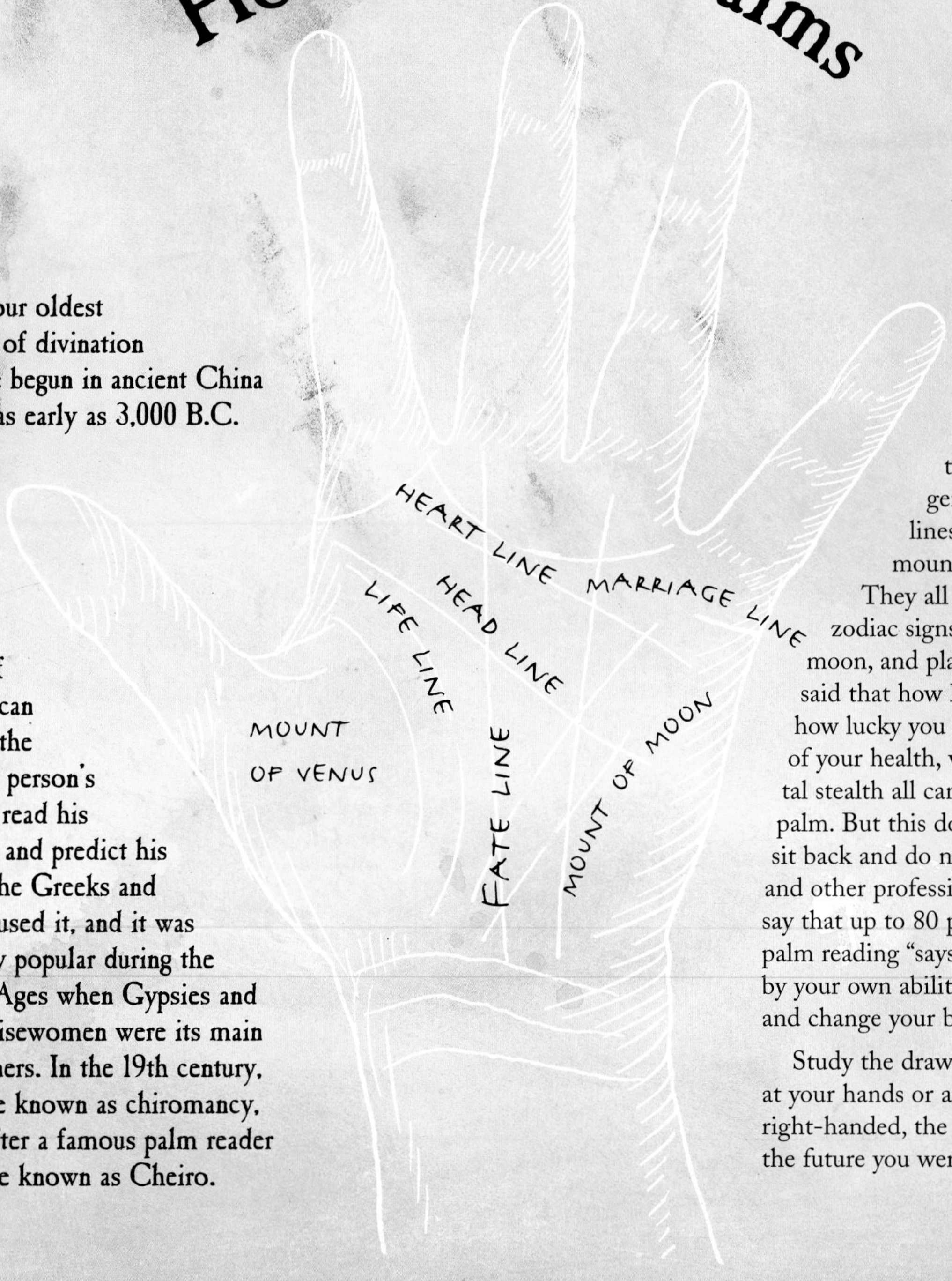

One of our oldest methods of divination may have begun in ancient China or India as early as 3,000 B.C. It's the art of palmistry, and it's based on the belief that you can interpret the lines in a person's hands to read his character and predict his future. The Greeks and Romans used it, and it was especially popular during the Middle Ages when Gypsies and village wisewomen were its main practitioners. In the 19th century, it became known as chiromancy, named after a famous palm reader of the age known as Cheiro.

HEART LINE

HEAD LINE

LIFE LINE

MARRIAGE LINE

FATE LINE

MOUNT OF MOON

MOUNT OF VENUS

How is it done?

A reader looks at the shape of the hands and fingers, and at the lines, digits, and mounds of the palms. They all correspond to zodiac signs and to the sun, moon, and planets. I've heard it said that how long you'll live, how lucky you are, and the state of your health, wealth, and mental stealth all can be read in your palm. But this doesn't mean you sit back and do nothing! Wizards and other professional palm readers say that up to 80 percent of what a palm reading "says" can be changed by your own ability to make choices and change your behavior.

Study the drawing and then look at your hands or a friend's. If you're right-handed, the left hand shows the future you were born with, and

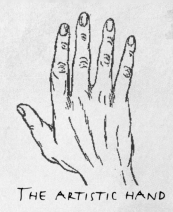

THE ARTISTIC HAND

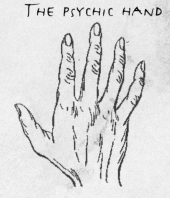

THE PSYCHIC HAND

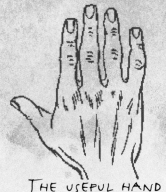

THE USEFUL HAND

the right hand shows how successful you've been in realizing your destiny.

If you're left-handed, your right hand shows the future you were born to, and the left hand shows your success in realizing your destiny. Deep, clear lines belong to someone who lives her life with gusto, feeling great happiness and sometimes sadness. Faint lines mean a person should Get a Life!

Smooth skin indicates a refined, energetic, and flexible nature. Long fingers and hands and pointed fingertips show artistic talent and a thoughtful nature. A broad, square hand indicates a strong, practical person who enjoys activity. Gentle, idealistic people have long fingers. Tapering fingers mean a person is inclined to extremes, and round or flat fingers mean they're the outdoorsy type. Look at the thumb. A long center bone means a person is very rational, but a short top bone means he doesn't have much willpower!

The Life Line is the most important line in your palm. You can divide it into approximate time periods of your life. Starting where the

Life Line is near the Head Line, the first third represents the first 25 years of your life, the next third the next 25 years, and the last third the final span of your life.

If you see another line closer to the Mount of Venus that runs parallel to the Life Line, you have good luck and lots of energy in your favor. You're ambitious if the Life Line rides high on your hand, and generous if it circles into your palm. There are tiny lines that connect the Life and Head Lines. They indicate you'll reach important goals at certain times of your life, depending on where they reach the Life Line. A triangle created by the Life Line and two tiny lines means you have a special talent that will be very satisfying, if you discover it and pursue it.

Compare the Head and Heart Lines, because the way they relate to each other tells a lot about a person. If one line is longer than the other, that indicates whether the person tends to be intellectual, or emotional and intuitive about things. If the Head Line is long and deep, the person is really smart! If a powerful Head Line slants downward, the

person should be careful in choosing the right goals for the best use of his talents. A prominent Heart Line means that, when that person feels, he feels very deeply. A short Heart Line means you'll have lots of boyfriends or girlfriends.

A full and deeply marked Fate Line means success and popularity. If it stops at the Head Line, that person needs to overcome a tendency to think too long about an opportunity without taking action. If the Fate Line breaks at the Heart Line, the person allows emotion to get in the way of good fortune.

The Marriage Line or lines don't mean how many times you'll get married. It shows how many times we will care so deeply for someone that the memory will stay with us for the rest of our lives. The Mount of Venus, if it's full and warm, means this person can be a good, kind friend.

A well-developed Mount of the Moon means a person is both imaginative and practical. And finally, if there are lines forming a triangle on the Mount of the Moon, that person could be psychic!

FAREWELL from the Wizard

Well, you've stayed the course and reached the end of this book of mine. You've read about wizards and much else that came before you, and you're busily making most of the things you need to become a wizard yourself. You must be wondering, what else could this old man possibly have to say?

I hope my *Book of Wizard Craft* has delighted you. I hope you feel proud of the crafts you've learned and the things you've made with your own hands. I hope my insider's tales about being a wizard have been helpful or at least good for a laugh. And I hope that you've gotten a delicious shiver or two from some of the things I've written in these pages. Life's goodness always feels sweeter and more precious to us when we're aware of its dark and mysterious paths.

If there's one last thought I want to leave with you, it is "Use Your Powers!" It would be a grave mistake if you never used the special talents inside you that are just bursting to get out. Everyone's got them. So pay attention to the things that make you curious and give you happiness. They're clues to your true wizard's nature.

I will enjoy watching your progress, even though I'll soon be in a place and time not accessible to mortals. But you never know, I may come back for a visit now and again out of sheer curiosity. Someday, you might pass a cloaked stranger on the street. Was that a wink you just saw? Don't stop. Just smile to yourself, and think of it as my way of saying hello. FROM ONE WIZARD TO ANOTHER.

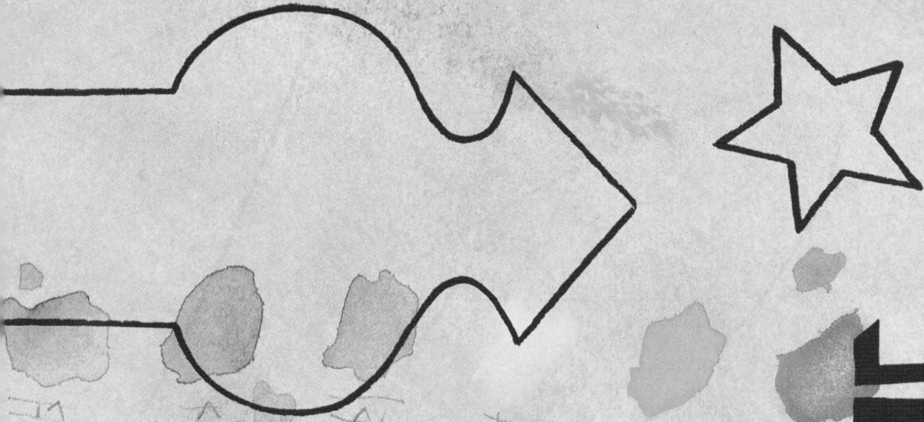

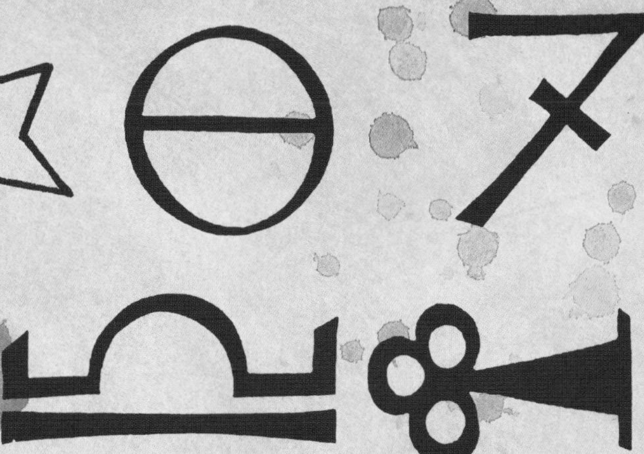

TEMPLATES
for Wizard Crafts

Copy or trace these templates to help
decorate your wizard crafts.

ENLARGE THESE BATS AND STARS 300%

FOR THE PROJECT ON PAGE 52.

ALCHEMICAL
SYMBOLS FOR
DECORATING
YOUR ROBE,
YOU'LL
PROBABLY WISH
TO ENLARGE
THEM...
(PAGES 16
AND 17)

HINGE TEMPLATES FOR YOUR SECRET
JOURNAL...SEE PAGE 92.

Use these design templates for the Crystal Ball on page 53.

Minaret template for magic carpet, page 46.

Enlarge the mask and beak templates to fit your face for the Great Horned Owl mask on page 120.

Enlarge to fit on your rug, probably around 500%.

Decorate your Toad garden castle with these patterns, see page 88.

To make the Spinning Snake project on page 135, enlarge this pattern 200%.